D1644124

CAREER ON COURSE

10 STRATEGIES TO TAKE YOUR CAREER FROM ACCIDENTAL TO INTENTIONAL

SCOTT JEFFREY MILLER

BakerBooks
a division of Baker Publishing Group
Grand Rapids, Michigan

Published by Baker Books
a division of Baker Publishing Group
Grand Rapids, Michigan
www.bakerbooks.com

Printed in the United States of America

Library of Congress Cataloging-in-Publication Data
Names: Miller, Scott Jeffrey, author.
Title: Career on course : 10 strategies to take your career from accidental to intentional / Scott Jeffrey Miller.
Description: Grand Rapids, Michigan : Baker Books, a division of Baker Publishing Group, [2024] | Includes bibliographical references.
Identifiers: LCCN 2023022901 | ISBN 9781540903426 (cloth) | ISBN 9781493443314 (ebook)
Subjects: LCSH: Vocational guidance.
Classification: LCC HF5381 .M494 2024 | DDC 650.1—dc23/eng/20230722
LC record available at https://lccn.loc.gov/2023022901

Some names and identifying details have been changed to protect the privacy of individuals.

Baker Publishing Group publications use paper produced from sustainable forestry practices and post-consumer waste whenever possible.

24 25 26 27 28 29 30 7 6 5 4 3 2 1

CONTENTS

Introduction 5

STRATEGY 1: Know Your Professional Values 27

STRATEGY 2: Decide If You're a Specialist or a Generalist 57

STRATEGY 3: Study Yourself 71

STRATEGY 4: Illustrate and Recalibrate Your Long-Term Plan 95

STRATEGY 5: Define and Build Your Brand 117

STRATEGY 6: Be Willing to Disrupt Yourself 133

STRATEGY 7: Take the Lead with Your Leader 153

STRATEGY 8: Do the Job You Were Hired For, Plus the One You Want 169

STRATEGY 9: Keep Your Ear to the Ground 185

STRATEGY 10: Dig Your Well Before You're Thirsty 199

Conclusion 211

Bonus Strategy: Own Your Development 219

Notes 221

INTRODUCTION

You're going to get to know me quite well over the next fifty thousand words. And for that I apologize.

I've had a remarkable career. Truly, it's been an exceptional professional journey by nearly every standard. This doesn't mean I haven't experienced my share of setbacks, surprises, and even missteps. I've been hired and fired. I've been promoted and demoted. And through these successes and failures, I've learned a tremendous amount about how to build, sustain, and take intentional control of one's career. And, of course, I didn't get there on my own. I've been the recipient of a long line of leaders who coached me, modeled great behaviors for me to emulate, and encouraged me to both maximize and minimize areas I saw as perceived strengths.

Now, nearly thirty-five years into my career journey, I've come to realize one shockingly consistent challenge everyone seems to face. And that's the subconscious abdication of their career, depending upon the accidental rather than carving out an intentional set of strategies and owning it fully. Sadly, this abdication is a pervasive commonality I've seen among otherwise exceptionally talented professionals who don't understand why their career isn't gaining traction, feels episodic, or isn't culminating in the financial success, level of influence, or sense of mission and purpose they had hoped it would.

After looking at hundreds of careers and conducting equal numbers of formal and informal interviews, I came to discern the vital need to move from accidental to intentional in one's career. Most of my interviewees claimed to be intentional, but when gently pressed they admitted they weren't. I also found a consistent level of responsibility and deliberateness around those who had managed a successful career—often at a level they didn't even recognize. Sure, they likely benefited from some degree of serendipity along the way, but it was more of an outlier than a dependency. And so I've made this the topic of my seventh book in the hopes of helping you move from accidental to intentional in your own career.

Which isn't to say your career is *everything* that matters. It's certainly not your source of life, identity, or self-worth. Each of these is worthy of your time, attention, and personal investment. But it would be a mistake to believe you can completely separate the personal from the professional, nor should you assume they are one and the same.

Crafting an intentional career matters; leaving it to chance will almost certainly diminish your levels of joy and accomplishment and the legacy you leave behind.

Whether you're newly placed in your first real job, know the ropes a bit but want to feel in greater control of your larger career arc, on a precipice in your career journey, or even late in the game and considering your final pivot or two, I've written this book for you. Because chances are we're not so different, except I'm likely a few steps ahead in my career journey. And looking back, there are things I wish others had told me decades ago about how to navigate the complexities of a meaningful career and how to become the architect of a career course.

Today, I think of what would've been helpful for me to know and augment it through the lens of my own exploration of what leadership and meaningful careers look like. It's a perspective I've forged from my own experiences on the career front lines as well as through numerous interviews with today's most gifted thought and business leaders, including chief human resource officers, chief people officers, vice presidents of people services, directors of training and development, and a trove of recruiters, headhunters, and placement professionals. I can assure you I'm not locked away in some ivory tower poring through academic journals, engaged in philosophical flights of fancy, or bending to whatever trend may seem momentarily in vogue. I've experienced the long arc of a professional career firsthand, working my way up from a college intern to a member of the C-suite of a publicly traded global company. Been there. Done that. Got the T-shirt. Now I have specific lessons to teach you as a result.

For example, I'll share how to take better, if not complete, control of your entire multidecade career so that you're better prepared for life after your work. Not just at the very end, but at the end of each day. This is the essence of creating an intentional strategy for your career so that you own and dictate it as opposed to allowing someone else to do so.

Over a decade ago, I overhead an executive say something profound.

And offensive.

And yet also true.

She pitched this idea in a room of her peers, and I was stunned: "You're never in the room when your career is decided for you."

At the time, I thought this was both sad and depressing but also piercingly insightful. Most of us unknowingly abdicate our careers to other people. Our bosses. Human resources and people services. And worse, the CFO who gives a new fiscal year budget to your team or division leader that's less than it was last year. Something or someone has to go.

This doesn't have to describe your career.

The Ten Strategies

I don't want another person to have their career decided by anyone other than themselves. Certainly, there are external forces beyond your control, but those should be rare—maybe occurring once or twice in your whole career. Mergers and acquisitions happen that create efficiencies and result in redundancies. That's just a reality. Recessions happen too, pretty much like clockwork, and roles must be eliminated to ensure the survival of organizations. Industries rise, peak, fall, and sometimes even disappear. And candidly some should. Like vaping, coal, cilantro, and truffle oil—four things we should all live without.

This book is about creating a deliberate, mostly impenetrable career where you thoughtfully lead your own plan. It's segmented into ten strategies I've developed, based on my research and my own experience, to create a proven process for charting an intentional career that has an extraordinary impact on your success when you master it:

1. Know your professional values.
2. Decide if you're a Specialist or a Generalist.
3. Study yourself.
4. Illustrate and recalibrate your long-term plan.
5. Define and build your brand.
6. Be willing to disrupt yourself.
7. Take the lead with your leader.
8. Do the job you were hired for, plus the one you want.
9. Keep your ear to the ground.
10. Dig your well before you're thirsty.

These ten strategies are purposely and carefully sequenced and come with work for you to do. I encourage you to take the time to complete the exercises located at the end of each chapter. Some will take hours, and others may take days or even weeks if done thoughtfully. Doing so will help you not only retain what you learned but put the various elements of each strategy into practice. There is, however, a single undergirding competency you should be aware of that permeates all the strategies in this book: *intentional careers are built on a foundation of self-awareness that improves strong communication and relationship skills.*

A Foundation of Self-Awareness

Allow me to address a specific professional skill everyone needs to master regardless of industry, level of education, role or title, age, or current technical prowess. I've interviewed many C-suite members, often founders and owners, from an array of companies and industries, and I've asked them all the same question: "What skill do you think is most needed in new associates entering your organization?"

Without fail, these highly experienced leaders all offered what amounted to the same response: *effective communication and relationship skills*.

Even leaders with an entirely virtual workforce or those focused on data and science place effective communication at the top of their list. It's now become a kind of game to me to see if someone I speak with on either of my two podcasts will answer the question differently. But even if I find a competent C-suite guest who might have lower energy, a stronger introverted personality, is perhaps more serious than I wished, or comes across as a strong left-brainer, they never disappoint on this topic. Just when I think an engineer, operations expert, or financial type might say "artificial intelligence" or "data analytics," they end up, without fail, expressing that communication and relationship building are the top skills they need in every new hire and at every level.

Case in point: I recently interviewed Mike Fenlon, Chief Future of Work Officer, PwC (PricewaterhouseCoopers), and he referred to communication and relationship skills as "power skills." I think most would agree that there's been a bias against such "soft skills" as compared to the perceived value of "hard skills" in industry. But as this gentleman and all the other C-suite professionals I interviewed have recognized, such a dismissal is foolish.

Yes, the communication skills we were supposed to learn in kindergarten and elementary school, at home with our parents and siblings, playing kickball against both bullies and braggarts, or walking door-to-door looking for lawn mowing or babysitting gigs in middle school matter. In fact, they matter a lot. So much so that we should think of them as power skills. As such, I've injected these communication and relationship skills throughout all ten strategies, often against a backdrop of more tactical career advice. I encourage you to keep such power skills in the back of your mind as you work to put your career on the course of your choosing. They include:

- Emotional intelligence
- Collaboration
- Interpersonal communication
- Adaptability
- Creativity
- Critical thinking
- Intercultural fluency
- Time management
- Active listening
- Conflict management
- Empathy
- Negotiation
- Problem-solving
- Teamwork

This list may seem like a list of competencies found in a job description, and that's exactly the point! Such power skills are the top competencies the most discriminating leaders are looking for. But what can be especially disheartening—and why I make self-awareness such a prominent theme throughout this book—is that we tend to overestimate the number of these skills we possess and our efficacy at deploying them.

In my nearly thirty-five-year career I've had the honor of interviewing hundreds of job candidates, starting as a team leader when I worked at a bakery and restaurant during high school, then as an executive officer of a global, public company, and now as an entrepreneur owning my own business. These interviews were my springboard for hiring hundreds of people. I then watched most of these hires as their careers either took flight or, in many cases, I had to let them go—despite their highly technical skills and competence in their respective areas of expertise—as their careers imploded.

My profound takeaway from this experience is this: when a career implodes or veers off course, it usually stems from a person's inability to communicate or get along well with others or from a lack of character or self-regulation.

Rarely is it from a lack of technical ability.

These employees simply didn't understand what it was like to work with and for them, so they had no concept of how difficult they were to be around, have a normal conversation with, or meet and collaborate with on a project. None of them in my experience were bad people, but they fundamentally lacked self-awareness and became drains on the culture, morale, and performance of their teams. As a result, they had to leave. Or more precisely, *we* had to leave them.

Against such a backdrop, you'll understand why I devote time in a career book like this one to topics such as self-awareness, building relationships, listening, resolving disputes, apologizing, seeking third alternatives, and effectively communicating ideas to others. I don't ever want you to find yourself walking into a conference room to see both your boss and someone from human resources waiting for you, ready to disclose the details of your severance package. For many, this experience can be so gut-wrenching that it's not uncommon to break down and start crying on the spot.

The alternative is to build yourself a foundation of self-awareness that improves strong communication and relationship skills as you work to be intentional about your career. And, to the extent that's possible, to put your career on the course of your choosing. That doesn't mean disruptions won't happen, but it can mean the difference between knowing how to quickly and effectively use your "map" to navigate back on course versus feeling lost, adrift, and without direction. And yes, it may seem at times like we're revisiting some of the power skill basics we should have gleaned from the school playground, but better that than engaging in the ill-fated career game "Red Rover, Red Rover, send HR on over."

Top Fives

Before we launch into our ten strategies, allow me to share one more insight that sits outside the rubric of any single strategy but should be helpful in the formation of your intentional career—the top five reasons people

- get hired
- get fired
- get promoted

The Top Five Reasons People Get Hired

From my research and experience, these are the top five reasons people get hired:

1. They are engaging.
2. They focus on what they can do for the organization, not what the organization can do for them.
3. They have an established track record.
4. They don't hide their gaps.
5. They have a history of grit and determination.

1. They are engaging.

I call this your BBQ factor. Ask yourself, *Would I make a great guest at a friend's BBQ? Am I a good conversationalist? Do I have varied interests and can I converse about a broad variety of topics? What's my personality like?*

You don't need to be the life of the party everywhere you go, but you need to add to and not subtract from the energy and engagement in the room. Further ask, *Would they invite me back? Why? If the leadership team was going to Top Golf on the day of my interview, how well would I fit in? Especially if I don't play golf?* (By the way, I don't—can't—play golf. But I can hit a ball off a tee, and even when I miss six times, I can laugh at myself, cheer others on, and change the topic to how much I love the chicken wings and thank everyone for inviting me.)

Revisiting a recurring theme and question in this book, How easily can you become comfortable being uncomfortable? Did you accept the invitation immediately? Did you bring a housewarming gift? Did you offer to help set up and clean up? How did you add to the conversation and participate in whatever the host organized? Did you send a thank-you note? Whether these are literal or metaphorical questions—hint: they're both—do some reflection on how easily likable you are, without changing who you are to please others. I'm not afraid to admit I don't fish, drink beer, or like hockey, NASCAR, or camping. But I can talk about them all and participate as needed to ensure my BBQ factor is high.

2. They focus on what they can do for the organization, not what the organization can do for them.

This reason was consistently told to me by recruiters, headhunters, and human resource and talent development leaders. When you're interviewing for a new position or a promotion, focus obsessively on what you uniquely bring to the role. How have you differentiated yourself with talents, skills, and passions to authentically convince the company interviewer that you genuinely want to progress their goals and help ensure success as they have defined it?

Of course, this is always a delicate balance as "power" shifts from the recruiter to the recruited. You will have plenty of time to illustrate your needs, ask self-serving questions, and determine if the fit is right for you. But let your overarching goal during the recruiting process be a focus on intimately understanding what success looks like in the role and how it connects to the company or organization's goals, and be masterful at articulating how you are the right person to make that happen. For them. The "for you" part will follow, I promise, if you first get the other part right.

3. They have an established track record.

Note what countless professional interviewers say about getting hired: do the job you were hired for first. Nothing gets someone hired and promoted faster than proven results in past roles. You either did or did not deliver or overdeliver on exactly what was entrusted to you by your previous leader. It really shouldn't be open to much debate, and you should be able to articulate your deliverables simply and eloquently. This includes what you did independently, in collaboration with a team, across business units, with clients, and with vendors. Be sure you acknowledge the contributions of others while you're stating your own results. And here's a bonus that will dramatically improve your brand: state the highest value information in the fewest number of words. Concise delivery of results is refreshing.

"I led the launch of six back-to-back product releases, with five of them exceeding the first ninety-day revenue projections."

"I maintained nine out of ten patient satisfaction ratings sixty-seven times in a row."

"In my four years in the sales role, I led the scoreboard for thirty-one months by having met or exceeded my assigned sales quota."

Be sure to speak specifically with measurables while you use language relatable to their industry, in their organization, and within their culture.

4. They don't hide their gaps.

Here's a great story that says it all: I once interviewed a gentleman in his thirties for a sales position. I'd worked with him a decade earlier, and his performance had been acceptable. Not stellar but also not concerning. He'd left the company for several years and was interviewing again for a sales position that happened to be the same one he'd left years earlier. The company, offerings, business model, and go-to-market strategy had changed enough that his hiring wasn't a slam dunk. And there were numerous other equally qualified candidates to choose from.

As I was interviewing him, I noticed on his résumé a period of about eighteen months during which he wasn't employed in sales but had taken on a position as a laborer. Having interviewed countless people that year, I was well aware that the recent recession had displaced vast swaths of people professionally. I pointedly asked him why he hadn't worked in sales during those months. His response to me was, nearly word-for-word, "Scott, I lost my sales role in a sweeping downsizing and looked desperately for a role in the industry—any industry—and couldn't find anything. I had a family to feed, so I went to work painting fences for a neighbor who fortunately hired me. I painted fences outside for nearly two years because I had obligations to my family. I didn't have any other choice."

I hired him back on the spot.

Not because of sympathy but rather because of his transparency and proven work ethic to do whatever it took to get the job done.

5. They have a history of grit and determination.

Would you have painted fences? How long would it have taken you to pivot?

One of my favorite lessons learned from working with Dr. Stephen R. Covey is a mantra he often repeated: "Use your R and your I." This meant using your resourcefulness and your initiative. It's a phrase I've drilled into our three young sons when they lament (hourly) that they can't find their shoes, backpacks, or toothbrushes. When you deploy your own resourcefulness and initiative, you can get nearly anything done.

Ask yourself, *How easily do I feel defeated? What's my history of throwing in the towel?* I can't think of a single time I've done either. I'm like a Weeble. Remember those little toys from the '70s that always sat up straight by using their egg-shaped design combined with gravity? They came with the catchy song, "Weebles wobble but they don't fall down." Millions and millions were sold. Forgive this trip down memory lane, but my advice here is simple: become a Weeble and refuse to fall down, no matter how hard you're pushed.

The Top Five Reasons People Get Fired

Consider now the top five reasons, in my experience, people get fired:

1. They lack judgment.
2. They have a lack of self-awareness.
3. They lack character.
4. They don't contribute.
5. They have a victim mentality.

1. They lack judgment.

I think good judgment is best defined as possessing self-regulation. Do you have the ability to resist always saying what's on your mind, out loud, to and in front of others?

Do you have the self-regulation to keep your emotions in check? It means dropping the profane language from the tip of your tongue. Resisting the tirade you genuinely feel the person across the conference room deserves (all while other people in the meeting are texting to encourage you to let it rip). Ignoring the temptation to tell everyone what you really think of them, the strategy, the product, your customers, and your boss.

Giving in to such base instincts can feel great in the moment—trust me, I've been there—but the price you pay later is rarely worth it. Instead, develop the judgment and self-regulation to ask yourself, *Will this person think it's as funny as I do? Will they find this as entertaining as it was when I role-played it in my head? Does this person have different boundaries, fears, or experiences than I do? Should I resist saying or doing what feels very right in the moment but may be very wrong in the long run?*

2. They have a lack of self-awareness.

Isn't it interesting that a lack of self-awareness came up as a key reason people lose their jobs? Continue to ask yourself the following questions throughout your career and life:

- What's it like being in any kind of relationship with me?
- What's it like to be my tennis or pickleball partner?
- What is my percentage of talking versus listening in my interpersonal relationships?
- How often do I interrupt or one-up someone else's story or experience?

- Can I be serious when needed? Can I relax and be jovial when needed?
- Do I dominate conversations or hold back so much that nobody can ever predict my position?
- Am I comfortable maturing and evolving my personality as needed in different situations?
- Can I read the body language and emotions of others and adjust as needed?

3. They lack character.

This is simple. Don't lie. Don't steal. Don't cheat.

In addition, understand and respect the company's or organization's stated policies and standards and don't cross them. They're written in the manual to protect the company from any legal recourse when they fire someone for a legitimate infraction. Increasingly, employers are under pressure to exit otherwise valuable—even invaluable—associates when there's a breach of trust. Now more than ever, the common standard is "one strike and you're out." Don't make the fatal mistake of confusing your contribution with an allowance for bad behavior.

4. They don't contribute.

Typically, this falls into one of two camps. Either they truly don't deliver, as in they're incapable or unwilling to execute the requirements of their role, or they continually take credit for the work of others. And, unlike in years past, their colleagues will rat them out in an instant. As they should.

Every leader's biggest concern is retaining talent, especially their high performers. The quickest way to annoy your top producers is to allow mediocrity in others. Leaders who don't call out poor performers and deal with them swiftly risk diminishing not only their own credibility but also the respect and engagement of the top producers they don't want (and can't afford) to lose. So contribute—not only the minimum or exactly what your role demands from you, but beyond—to the overall team goal, to the culture, and to the success of those around you. Or leave.

5. They have a victim mentality.

We all know this person by their constant declarations that everyone is out to get them. Not only that, but the fates have conspired against them so that nothing goes their way. And on top of that, they simply have the worst luck. It's not their fault, of course. They're the unfortunate victim, unjustly so, to a world arrayed against them at every turn. It's always everyone else's fault. They never are responsible.

The victim is incapable of showing up with the required level of maturity and admitting when they're wrong or make a mistake.

The Top Five Reasons People Get Promoted

Finally, let me conclude with the top five reasons I've found people get promoted:

1. They get results.
2. They make themselves indispensable.
3. They help others outside of their role.
4. They put themselves in challenging situations.
5. They make others look good.

1. They get results.

See a theme here?

As a seven-time author and a literary agent, I'm frequently asked what the best way is to have a bestselling book. Is it the cover? The title? Great website? Huge social media following? Big publicity tour? Hiring a great agent to land your book at the best publishing house?

"Which of these things, Scott? Just tell me how much to spend and who to hire, and I will do whatever you tell me."

Here's what I tell everyone: "Just write an amazing book and it will sell. An amazing book. Not a great book. An amazing book."

Take that advice and apply it to your career. Deliver. Overdeliver. Exceed expectations. Do more than what's expected from you, and it will get recognized. And if it doesn't, the answer is simple—you're working for either the wrong leader or in the wrong organization. And you need to leave and find the right one.

2. They make themselves indispensable.

Depending on your exact career situation and the size of your team, unit, division, or company, I'd challenge you to take a few minutes and write down the name of everyone on your immediate team. Try to keep it to twenty or fewer people. I then want you to rank them all, including yourself, top to bottom, with respect to who would be terminated first, then second, and so on in the event of a major financial setback, such as the onset of another pandemic or a war, and only those who were absolutely indispensable could remain.

If the company had forty-eight hours to reduce head count by 70 percent, who would be first to be let go and who would be last? Look closely at where you place your name, and then figure out how to move down the list. Lower is better. Last is best. Do you own revenue? Do you own containing costs? Do you manage the most valuable clients in the company? What's your role, and how can you contribute so extraordinarily that you earn the last name on the list? Start making it happen.

3. They help others outside of their role.

These are the colleagues who have an abundance mentality. While simultaneously delivering on their own projects and commitments, they look around to support others. They're constantly scanning the organization to see who might need some help. Who is struggling? Who is on the rise and might benefit from some support? It's a mindset more than a skill set. This will look different for every role you're in and each organization you're associated with. Think about how to be so intentional about this that it becomes a part of your brand. It might be sharing information more generously or offering to be part of a brainstorming session for a division, product, or service that in no way benefits you or your own career. It might be sharing budget or other resources that you have responsibility for. Chew on this and put it into action. People will notice.

4. They put themselves in challenging situations.

This isn't just about accepting stretch goals but giving yourself opportunities to grow your skills beyond what even you think is reasonable. Be thoughtful not to place yourself in situations where you might trip up significantly and experience a major setback or tarnish your well-cultivated brand.

Calibrate. Let it be public knowledge that you're the go-to person for tough assignments. This might even involve a conversation with your leader or their leader in which you tell them how interested you are in growing, and that you realize the value of both delivering on your current commitments and taking on "one more"—one more project, one more direct report, one more client, one more assignment. I personally love the book *The Power of One More: The Ultimate Guide to Happiness and Success* by Ed Mylett. Do yourself a favor by reading it and absorbing everything Ed says.

5. They make others look good.

Lead up. Lead across. Lead down. The more you're known for lifting others, the more they will lift you. This is a principle in life. Practice it and make it your natural mindset. It reminds me of a quote from US president Harry S. Truman, who said, "It's amazing how much you can accomplish if you do not care who gets the credit."

What to Look Forward to in This Book

We've set the litmus test for an intentional career (that you love). We've acknowledged the need for strong communication and relationship skills (skip these and you'll fail miserably). And we've shared the top five reasons people get hired, fired, and promoted. The rest of this book will focus on the ten specific strategies for an intentional career along with vital exercises for each one.

Applying any single strategy can be powerful. But allow me to repeat an important point: take the time to complete the exercises following each strategy in the order in which they're presented. As you'll come to discover, many strategies build on others. To get the most out of this book—and subsequently out of your career— invest the time to do the work sequentially, thoughtfully, and thoroughly before proceeding to the next strategy. You'll thank me for this advice when you're done, believe me on this.

Connect with me anytime at ScottJeffreyMiller.com about questions, comments, or issues you're facing. We're friends now—let's support each other.

STRATEGY

Know Your Professional Values

At first blush, identifying your values may seem like a tired topic. Who hasn't, during times of professional or personal development, been invited to explore, identify, and live by their values? Well, that isn't the single theme of this chapter. Of course, identifying your values is essential, but I'll take it a step further by asking you to differentiate between your *personal* and *professional* values.

"But shouldn't they be one and the same?" you might be asking. "Shouldn't we all live by one pervasive set of values?"

The short answer is no. With the important caveat that although our goal is ideally to find *congruence* between our two sets of values, there will be times of conflict between them, and that's fine. But you can never uncover the cause of the conflict and decide whether or not to do something about it if you don't understand *why* there's conflict and accept the potential trade-offs. The fact is, there will be times of *incongruence* between your personal and professional values, and ultimately, it's up to you whether you choose to subjugate one to the other or accept the incongruence because it's driving a predetermined goal.

The career-changing insight I'll share in this chapter is that *how you intentionally flow between your personal and professional values will fundamentally influence the course your career takes*. This is something I've experienced firsthand.

In 2005, I was living in Chicago and working as the lead of my company's regional office, directing a team of about seventy-five colleagues spread across more than ten states. I was on top of the world as a single, well-paid, healthy professional with lots of friends and a reasonably balanced life. It wasn't uncommon for me to wake up on a Thursday morning and text a friend in Europe to tell them I'd meet them at the train station in Amsterdam, London, Rome, or Prague the next morning for three days of fun. Looking back now, I realize I lived my sixties in my thirties! Perhaps, had I known that at the time, I might have appreciated it more.

My career was on fire and, as a result, I was promoted beyond my skill set; read *The Peter Principle* by Laurence J. Peter for more on this phenomenon. Though impostor syndrome wasn't a label at the time, I was anxiously waiting to be exposed as a fraud. Welcome to most careers, especially when they're off course and you're bouncing from role to role, company to company, and industry to industry.

Somehow, I'd managed to dupe everyone into thinking our region's success was "just around the corner" while the executive leadership had bigger issues to work on than "that guy Scott out in Chicago." I hung on for six years, then finally saw the writing on the wall. I could see my time was almost up in that specific role, so I intentionally disrupted myself and found a different position in the company and started my way up to the C-suite. Can you believe it—from the front line to the C-suite of a global, public company in ten years? (More on *that* replicable skill in Strategy 6.)

Sometime nearing the end of my sales leadership tenure in Chicago, I attended a company-wide conference where both founders were the keynote speakers. First up was Dr. Stephen R. Covey, author of *The 7 Habits of Highly Effective People*. Twenty years had transpired since he'd first released his seminal book, and our leadership development company, FranklinCovey, was booming worldwide.

One of Dr. Covey's popular contributions was the concept of writing a personal mission statement, or what he referred to as "Your own personal constitution," which was similar to what companies and organizations post on their walls and list in their annual reports. Dr. Covey advocated that defining a personal mission was vital to living an effective life.

As I'd worked in the firm for nearly a decade, this wasn't a new concept to me. I'd both sold and taught the principles of mission statements to numerous organizations, government entities, and educational institutions, helping them refine their own through extensive consulting and implementation plans. I found it invigorating and recognize even today, decades later, that the key to recruitment and retention centers around creating a mission and vision that associates can be galvanized by and connect to. Ask an übersatisfied employee why they love their job, and you're likely to hear one of several responses.

"I love my leader."

"I love the culture of my company."

"I love the contribution I'm making."

"I'm passionate about our mission."

Even prior to my self-disruption, I would've said the same about my professional experience. Which explains a twenty-five-year tenure in the same organization. I know . . . I'm a dinosaur. Or maybe not. Perhaps I'm just one of the fortunate few who've managed to fulfill nearly all their career ambitions in one organization—nine separate careers within one company. And when I say "fortunate," I also mean "intentional."

Yet the idea of a *personal* mission statement was still something that hadn't resonated with me. I was, after all, living large in my thirties and had no clue what my mission was or should be. My roles in life were few: leader and friend (mostly in that order, for good or bad). If you really pressed me at the time, I could've added son, brother, uncle, and third cousin to the mix, but as my parents had no living siblings, any family reunions would've amounted to a whopping eight people. So, it's understandable why I wasn't exactly on fire about determining my mission in life other than perhaps more dinner parties, more tennis, more European vacations, more cars, more clothes, and a general sense of just having more.

Shallow, maybe—but I was single and responsible to and for no one but me. Which meant the session with Dr. Covey was a bust for me, 100 percent *because* of me, and I made it through both unmoved and unscathed.

Then our other cofounder, Hyrum Smith, took the stage. Although less well-known globally than Dr. Covey, he was an icon in our company and in the time management industry as the modern "father of time management." In essence, he invented the Franklin Planner, the bestselling paper planning tool in history, inspired by Ben Franklin's own life and personal values. For me, he was a force of nature. Where Dr. Covey was a bit more academic, reserved, and cerebral,

Hyrum was the everyman. He was fun, energetic, vivacious, and a rock star storyteller. His passion and zest for life were contagious. And while I'm immensely grateful and inspired by Dr. Covey, Hyrum was my personal hero. Both Dr. Covey and Hyrum Smith have since passed away, but their legacies continue to impact the lives of millions of people around the world. Together, they created the conditions for me to chart an intentional career.

Back to the conference . . . one keynote down and one to go. Hyrum stepped up to speak and immediately implored everyone to get out a pad of paper and a pen—and launched into the speech of his life.

And mine.

The topic? Our values.

That day in Chicago, joined by over a thousand of my colleagues, my life was transformed. And as the adage goes, "When the student is ready, the teacher will appear." That was certainly the case for me. I'm not sure why the topic of values resonated with me when the similar theme of a personal mission statement didn't, but I suppose it was related to the fact that Dr. Covey spoke so prescriptively regarding the connection between roles and mission. And as I said, my roles at the time were few. Hyrum, however, challenged us to write out our values and then go live our lives in accordance with them. He was famous for saying that what all humans want in life is harmony and congruence between our identified values and how we choose to live our lives.

Later that day, I drove back to my loft apartment and went to work crafting my values. Now, to remind you, it wasn't like I'd never heard the concept of defining values before. But when it came to such introspection, I was a water-skier, not a diver, and I'd been skimming happily along the surface. So it took me some time and effort, and after four to five days of introspection and multiple drafts, I'd come up with a list of personal values that I thought were both meaningful to me and represented who I was and aspired to be.

I wasn't soulless after all. Just shallow.

Reflecting on my list, I was quite proud of the seven values I'd identified. Little did I know this short list of seven words would drive all my critical life decisions for decades to come. I'd taken Hyrum's challenge quite seriously, and something inside of me started burning brighter as I began the process of looking for more. Later, I'd learn that "more" was named Stephanie, my future wife, and our three sons: Thatcher, Smith, and Wentworth. So much for the single life, as two years later I was married at forty-one, and we had three boys in five years. Here, then, is my list of seven values that have shaped the ensuing nineteen years:

Purpose
Health
Integrity
Loyalty
Positivity
Abundance
Learning

Not exactly the *Magna Carta*, but I was pleased with my list, especially when I further recognized the individual words formed an acronym: PHILPAL. This meant I could remember them for longer than a day.

One of the insights I've come to understand since this experience with Hyrum is that too many people, when asked their values on the spot, spout off a series of words from the top of their head that sound good in the moment but lack meaning and commitment. Instead, Hyrum advocated, we should carefully craft our values based on what we want in life, what we believe, what we need, and what we want to offer. What we want our brand and reputation to be based on. We must disregard (or at least minimize) what anyone else needs or wants from us as we fight the temptation to impress by offering a string of ad hoc values aligning to whatever seems in vogue.

Most of us do just that if the topic comes up. I'm confident that if I gathered a hundred random people—including highly educated and successful professional leaders and independent contributors perhaps like you—and asked them their values, the majority would rattle off an extemporaneous list that may be beautifully delivered and momentarily relevant but would likely be different from their answer four months later. Or even four days later.

That's not a crime, but it's also not knowing your values.

Nor is a rote, memorized list enough either. How many of us were forced to memorize the Preamble to the US Constitution, the Pledge of Allegiance, or the Ten Commandments?

Check. Check. Check.

How many of us are daily living our lives aligned to them?

How much time have I personally spent deconstructing them and deeply pondering what the words actually mean? Not much, truthfully. And I think if you're honest, the same is true for you. I especially struggle with that ninth commandment. Can't recall which one that is? That's my point. So, let's work on breaking that pattern in life.

Determine Your Personal Values

The very first step in any successful, fulfilling, and intentional career is to determine your personal values. Don't worry, we'll get to professional values as advertised. This isn't done over a latte. Ten lattes, maybe . . . but my point here is it takes time to thoughtfully edit, revise, rethink, pressure-test, and confirm your list of personal values. They need to resonate with who you are, how you intend to put them into action, and what you're going to say yes or no to in life. Remember the adage: "Each time you say yes to something new, that just reinforces you have no real goals of your own." This will change how you look at your daily schedule and how you choose to spend and invest your time.

Any of us could likely make a defense to support our decisions if pressed, but that's the wrong test. A career (and life) in which you're in control of your time, happiness, purpose, and level of fulfillment is deeply rooted in, and connected to, a set of deliberately defined personal values. And it requires courage and maturity to accept the consequences (positive and negative) that flow from that alignment.

Thus, the first big idea of this book is to determine your personal values and strive to live in congruence with them. At this point, I invite you to take one of two next steps:

1. Stop reading here and skip to the end of this chapter to begin the process of defining your personal values, which might take hours or days. Nothing else in the book matters until you have those personal values identified and committed to your memory and actions.

2. Continue reading and finish this chapter for context on the equal importance of identifying your professional values, then begin both exercises.

Regardless, I implore you not to move to Strategy 2 until you've completed, or at least made substantial progress in, both Strategy 1 exercises. Yes, that may mean you delay reading beyond this chapter for a few days or weeks, and that's fine. I know there's a risk you might step out of the book, become lost in the articulation of your values, and get sucked back into your accidental career and never come back. That's a risk I'm willing to take.

Are you?

• • • • • •

Okay . . . it's either two seconds or two weeks later for you. Let's keep going.

Earlier, I mentioned my own personal values expressed as the acronym PHILPAL: purpose, health, integrity, loyalty, positivity, abundance, and learning. Now, these aren't just words I thought up that I hoped sounded impressive to others. In fact, just the opposite. Let me declare here, with the possibility of offending you, that I couldn't care less what you think about my values. They're mine, not yours. It's my life, not yours.

Maybe it's my age—this isn't something I could've truthfully said twenty years ago. I cared way too much and for way too long about what others thought about me. But I'm over it, and I invite you to accelerate your adoption of the same mindset. Similarly, a new refrain from many creators and influencers in the spotlight is "Your opinion of me is not my business."

This may have felt a little harsh to you. If so, mission accomplished. I want to deeply inculcate in you that your values should only matter to and impress one person—you. Having said that, for those of you who are married or in any committed relationship, it's likely that your partner's opinion about your values will have some level of impact and relevance. If anyone's opinion matters, it's theirs, as your values will almost certainly impact them the most in life. But your values do not need to perfectly mirror theirs, or vice versa.

Personal Values Framing Questions

As you contemplate your list of personal values, free from the concerns and judgments of others, consider the following:

- What are your current roles in life, and who have you made commitments to that you intend to keep?
- How much will those roles change in the near or short term that might impact your values?
- What is your mission? Your purpose in life? Do you even know it? Where are you on the ever-changing journey of trying to uncover it? Discover it? Create it?
- What brings you joy? Meaning? Happiness? These sound like words from a retreat-based journaling exercise that may not resonate with you. But as a guy further from his forties than his sixties, let me remind you how short life is. You should *absolutely* be able to name what brings you joy, meaning, and happiness—and your values should align to that.
- What is it you're trying to accomplish in your life? Have you set specific goals with a beginning and a

finish line? Furthermore, do you know when and how to celebrate your accomplishments?

- What do you want your legacy to be? What are you building as your reputation and brand?
- What's important to you? Why? What does that do for you and those whom you care about or are entrusted to protect and advance in their own lives?
- What are you grateful for? Who are you grateful for? Whose life do you admire and want to model your own authentic life after?

These are the types of questions you should be pondering as you engage in this vital life assignment. Sound like author hyperbole? Nope. Just sage advice from a dinosaur whose career and life have benefited disproportionately from this exercise.

I chose PHILPAL (purpose, health, integrity, loyalty, positivity, abundance, and learning) very deliberately to form my personal values, and I think most people who know me well could truthfully say I live closely aligned to them. What follows is a short description of each of my seven personal values in the hopes that it gives you some context and gravity for the weight values can play in your own personal and professional life moving forward.

Purpose. I'm still trying to determine what my purpose is. Until my Creator speaks more clearly to me about it or it's included in my eulogy, I think my life's purpose is now, as a father, to launch our three sons into an increasingly tough world as gentlemen with marketable professional skills, a mindset of kindness and respect to others, the confidence to seek and find happiness, and a differentiating work ethic that serves not only them but the world around them. My first value shows up in my daily life priorities and has grown and evolved with me. To this day, I still plan around it and find ways to honor it, elevate it, and defend it—while still struggling with it.

Health. This value is multifaceted and includes mental, social, emotional, and physical dimensions. I don't execute it perfectly—nor do I with any of my chosen values. But naming health as one of those values has certainly elevated it to a conscious level, and I absolutely make better lifestyle decisions because of it.

Integrity. I define this as doing my best to behave honorably when people are watching—and more importantly, when they're not. My litmus test is when I pass someone in a grocery store who knows me, and I imagine what they'll likely say about me to the person they're with once I'm out of earshot one aisle over.

Loyalty. I can confidently say I'm a fiercely loyal person. Often I'm loyal to a fault, but it never dissuades me—even if I get burned—from doing it again.

Positivity. Simply stated, I want my brand to be joyous and positive. Not so annoyingly that I can't relate to or even see many of the challenges we all face, but I like to see life through a lens of solutions, possibilities, and opportunities. What's the key to happiness in life? In my opinion it's simple: gratitude.

Abundance. The importance of living with a spirit of generosity and abundance has been deeply inculcated in me since I was a child. I try to share. Share credit. Time. Money. Goodwill. Praise. Things. Love. Attention. The stage and spotlight. I don't always get this right, which is why I made it a value. I want to be reminded of it daily.

Learning. Look to the bonus strategy Own Your Development for evidence that this is a personal value of mine.

Determine Your Professional Values

Hopefully running through my list of personal values was helpful for you. As you identify your own, think of it as simply the starting point for building an intentional life and career. What comes next is determining your professional values. And yes, they are different. After thirty years in the personal and professional development industry, I've never met anyone (except myself . . . how arrogant, I know) who took the work of articulating their personal values and expanded it to determine their professional values.

Authentically identifying what's important and valuable in your career will accelerate your ability to create a more intentional professional life. And often your two sets of values will feel at odds (not always incongruent but requiring that you emphasize one over the other for a period of time). This happens occasionally and situationally, but of all of the people whom I've coached and mentored in their careers, I can't name one who had enough clarity on both sets of values. As a result, they wonder why they're experiencing a "career cul-de-sac" or frustration at why their career isn't progressing as swiftly as or in the direction they want. It reminds me of a quote often attributed to the Cheshire Cat from *Alice's Adventures in Wonderland*: "If you don't know where you're going, any road will take you there."

If you were to say your top personal value is family but your top professional value is maximizing your income, that's likely to create some conflict. For example, I know very few fully commissioned salespeople who don't have to travel extensively. Yes, this may have changed some since the BC (Before COVID) era, but my sense is highly paid sales careers still require some level of face-to-face prospecting and client engagement. Which means if you're looking for upward momentum in your career via growing into sales leadership and overseeing individual sales contributors, you're going to likely live on a plane or in your car for long periods of time. Not in every case, but in most. That means missing the occasional music recital, soccer game, or even, regrettably, birthday.

Does that mean you have to give up entirely on either your family or maximizing your income? No. But it does mean you should recognize the conflict and own it. And realize your frustration may be an outcome of your intentional—not accidental—decisions. Maybe you'll need to allow one value to supersede another for a specific period. Maybe you'll need to make some short-term concessions to achieve your larger long-term goals. However you strike the balance, it's 100 percent your decision (which means you also own the consequences). Look forward and develop a plan for such tension in advance, rather than looking back with regret. Knowing when and why your values will come into conflict gives you the power to do something about it *now*. In effect, to create a plan. It also empowers you to stop blaming others (namely your leader) or external forces for your lack of momentum or acceleration.

Once I identified my personal values, I progressed to do the same professionally. This order is important because we often need the reminder that our careers aren't our lives. Lives first, careers second.

My professional values are less a list of words and more about concepts and phrases. They are:

- Maximize my income.
- Associate with an organization and brand I'm proud of.
- Work with people I like and respect and feel valued by.

My professional values reflect the fact that I work to earn money. That's a *duh*, I know, but I'm quite comfortable writing it here and even saying it in public, especially to my boss. I strive for the freedom and options that money provides me and my family. I'm in no way ashamed to say I value money above all else professionally—but not if it means selling illegal narcotics or working with thugs and thieves. And not if it means working for a company I'm ashamed of with people I distrust and dislike. Yes, income first, but not at all costs.

Finding Congruence between Personal and Professional Values

I could certainly have made more money in life if "maximizing my income" was my only professional value and I didn't care how incongruent it would be with my personal values. An intentional career as I've defined it, however, requires that we seek clarification and congruence between what we value personally and professionally. Clarifying both sets of values will

- lessen your impulsivity in decision-making,
- minimize the frequency of making career jumps that turn out to be bad decisions, and
- empower you to run more intentionally toward what you want and away from what you don't want.

The ebb and flow of personal and professional values is about the decision to sometimes lean into one more heavily than the other for a defined season. It is *not* about abandoning one set in favor of the other. Owning the outcomes of your intentional decisions prevents you from living a life of blame, victimhood, and frustration.

A Case Study in Values

Recently a colleague came to me about a crossroads in her career. Tina told me she was greatly conflicted about staying with her current employer or accepting one of two very lucrative offers from other organizations. By all accounts she had a stellar career, most of which had unfolded and blossomed through her current employer. She wasn't unhappy per se, just unsettled. In fact, most high performers are easily unsettled and don't tolerate perceived complacency in themselves or team members.

Tina went on to confide in me all the reasons she was leaning toward leaving, but she was also mindful of the reasons she should stay. I listened intently to an extensive download from her and then, after a pause, asked her rather practically what her professional values were.

Now, Tina isn't an ambivalent person and is what some would even call an overachiever. She excels at everything, drawing from an indefatigable work ethic. She is überdisciplined, intellectually rigorous, socially courageous, and a lifelong learner. Not surprisingly, she was being recruited by other companies who had made multiple offers. But when I asked her to state for me her professional values, she paused before delivering, with characteristic confidence, "I value working on a high-performance team and upward mobility." In other words, she wanted to work with people who were more committed to quality and performance than her current colleagues. She also wanted to be promoted to a vice president position.

I let that sit for a moment, validated what she said to me, and then pushed a bit. "Tina, I'm guessing you've not put a lot of thought into the question I just asked you, and that's okay, as most people haven't. But from what I know about you, I'm not convinced the professional values you stated are accurate or are fully representative of what you really want and value in your career. You've stated several times to me during this conversation that you think you can make more money by jumping ship, but interestingly, that didn't show up in your stated values. I'm guessing that might be because you thought I may judge you on that. After all, we both know you're currently the highest paid salesperson, by far, in your current company. And you deserve it. You've earned every dollar through your skills and work ethic. So, can I ask where income factors into your set of professional values?"

She considered this as I continued. "Further, I know you're the sole income earner in your family. You've shared with me before that you have a clear vision of what kind of life you want to live and the opportunities you want for your three young children. I also know you provide financially for extended members of your family. I don't want to steer you toward anything, but before you answer, remember I'm asking about *your* values. Not mine, not your husband's, not your current leader's, not anyone else's. Yours alone. And you shouldn't care what anyone, namely me, thinks about them. You decide. Period."

If I had been starring in one of those TV courtroom dramas, I would've looked into the camera and declared, "Your honor, the defense calls no further witnesses and rests its case." I knew her well enough to believe we'd gotten to the heart of the matter.

After some intense eye contact, she finally replied, "You're absolutely right, Scott. Income is in fact my top professional value."

"So there you have it," I continued. "Your number one professional value is to maximize your income. Your number two professional value is to work on a high-performance team, and your number three value is upward mobility. Specifically, you want a vice president title and to earn your way onto an executive leadership team."

With a bit of a grin she answered, "That's right."

The next day she offered her three weeks' notice. Talk about a professional taking control of her career and acting with extraordinary intentionality. All through the lens of knowing her personal and professional values. Following this same practice has saved me from making colossal mistakes in my own career and allowed me to counsel countless friends and colleagues to make more intentional career decisions.

EXERCISE SETUP

Know Your Professional Values

Our values provide a road map for how we treat others as well as establish the foundation for our reputation and legacy. Like people, most organizations have values. These are usually found in the employee handbook, referenced at town hall meetings, or etched somewhere at headquarters. And while some might believe organizations only give lip service to these, that's increasingly not the case. Today's conscientious organizations are increasingly identifying, promoting, and aligning colleagues with their stated values—hiring, advancing, and terminating accordingly.

For the individual, professional values are only meaningful when they're rooted in personal values. The resulting congruence or healthy tension between the two requires a thoughtful plan, balancing one over the other for a defined season, seeking to minimize rather than eliminate tension.

I'd like to reiterate how valuable I think the following exercise is. You will revisit this, if not annually, then certainly many times in your career, especially as your roles in life change. Values often change in alignment to roles. Raising young children usually correlates to different personal values than taking care of your elderly parents. Your professional values in your thirties will likely be different from those in your fifties. Please don't race through this exercise. Return to it at pivotal points in your life and career.

But first, let's talk about that healthy tension known to many as *conflict*.

When Your Values Are in Conflict

I'd like to offer some clarity about when your personal and professional values are in conflict. When we think of conflict, it typically connotes negativity. Someone wins or loses. There is triumph or defeat. But not all conflict is bad. Sometimes it's insightful, piercingly so, and can lead to clarity and resolution.

When you finish your two lists and have a contemplative opportunity to step back and look them over, you should invest some time in drawing connections as to how they may or may not be supporting the life you want to live. I've encountered far too many professionals who lack the wisdom and insight to see and take ownership of where and why their career is stumbling or outright faltering. Common targets for blame are the incompetence of their leader, the organizational culture, misaligned systems, poor strategies, or unremarkable products, or further external factors like a challenging economic environment or governmental policy. At some point in your career, all of these factors may be present. But what's also true is that you have little to no control over most of them.

Likely, any stagnation in your career may well be because your professional pursuits conflict with your professional values—or what is more often the case, your personal and professional values conflict with each other. Remember, that's not always a bad thing. It's a time for you to reflect on *why* there's conflict. Perhaps your personal roles (and thus values) need to supersede your professional values for a certain time.

For example, now that I'm in my fifties, married, and the father of three sons, and my mother is in her mideighties, my personal roles and values are increasingly in conflict with my own top professional value of maximizing my income. My family's needs require some serious coin, and as I'm an author and keynote speaker the coin only comes in when I'm on a plane, away from my family. You see the conflict. I have to assess these competing values constantly and ensure that I don't blame anyone else for their conflict.

I think the greatest outcome of this chapter's exercise is comparing your two final lists, looking for alignments and conflicts, and then determining what, if anything, you intend to do about any conflict—including nothing other than owning it.

Identify Your Personal and Professional Values

- For possible inspiration, think of people you admire and imagine what their personal or professional values might be. Pick no more than eight values in each category, as it's likely too difficult to act on any more than that. Rank them so you know which values might supersede others, if needed.
- If possible, create an acronym for each value category to recall them when faced with important decisions.
    - PHILPAL, my personal values acronym, has been guiding me ever since the fateful day when Hyrum Smith challenged us to define and live up to them. (PHILPAL stands for purpose, health, integrity, loyalty, positivity, abundance, and learning.)
    - My professional values are (1) Maximize my financial income, (2) Associate with an organization and brand I'm proud of, and (3) Work in a culture with people I like and respect and feel valued by. As there are only three, I don't feel the need for an acronym. But I guess it could be MAW!
- Keep in mind that your values may change over time. Expect such change and embrace it when it happens. Since you're evolving, your values may too.
- Resist selecting any value based on what anyone else thinks.
- Invest the time you need to define and commit to memory your personal and professional values. They're the lenses through which you will make your decisions and move from an accidental to an intentional career.

Know Your Personal Values

STEP 1: FIRST PASS

Circle or mark the words that best describe your PERSONAL values.

- O Abundance
- O Acceptance
- O Accountability
- O Adaptability
- O Agility
- O Authenticity
- O Autonomy
- O Balance
- O Bravery
- O Calmness
- O Community
- O Compassion
- O Connection
- O Conservation
- O Cooperation
- O Courage
- O Curiosity
- O Daringness
- O Decency
- O Decisiveness
- O Dedication
- O Dependability
- O Dignity
- O Diplomacy
- O Discretion
- O Diversity
- O Duty
- O Education
- O Empathy
- O Enlightenment
- O Equality
- O Fairness
- O Faith
- O Family
- O Fitness
- O Freedom
- O Friendship
- O Frugality
- O Fun
- O Generosity
- O Grace
- O Gratitude
- O Happiness
- O Hard work
- O Harmony
- O Health
- O Home
- O Honesty
- O Honor
- O Humility
- O Humor
- O Imagination
- O Inclusiveness
- O Innovation
- O Intimacy
- O Intuitiveness
- O Joy
- O Justice
- O Kindness
- O Knowledge

- O Leadership
- O Listening
- O Love
- O Loyalty
- O Meekness
- O Mindfulness
- O Moderation
- O Modesty
- O Nature
- O Optimism
- O Order
- O Partnership
- O Patience
- O Patriotism
- O Peace
- O Persistence
- O Personal dev.
- O Play
- O Preparedness
- O Proactivity
- O Prudence
- O Quality
- O Readiness
- O Relationship
- O Reliability
- O Renewal
- O Reputation
- O Resilience
- O Risk-taking
- O Safety
- O Security
- O Selflessness
- O Sensitivity
- O Service
- O Skillfulness
- O Spirituality
- O Spontaneity
- O Stability
- O Tactfulness
- O Temperance
- O Thankfulness
- O Thoroughness
- O Trust
- O Truth
- O Unity
- O Valor
- O Virtue
- O Vision
- O Wealth
- O Wellness
- O Wisdom
- O Work-life balance
- O ______________
- O ______________
- O ______________
- O ______________
- O ______________
- O ______________
- O ______________

Don't see a word you like? Fill in your own.

Take your time. It may take hours, days, even weeks to decide. This isn't a shopping list you rush to make before a trip to the store.

STEP 2: SHORT LIST

Choose your favorite values from step 1 and list them below.

- ____________________
- ____________________
- ____________________
- ____________________
- ____________________

STEP 3: MY PERSONAL VALUES

Tighten your list even more to finalize your values, and write them below.

- ____________________
- ____________________
- ____________________

STEP 4: VALUE BEHAVIORS

Describe what your values look like in your behaviors.

- ____________________
- ____________________
- ____________________

This is a narrowing process to help you finalize your personal values.

STEP 2:
SHORT LIST

- ______
- ______
- ______
- ______
- ______
- ______
- ______

STEP 3:
MY PERSONAL VALUES

- ______ →
- ______ →
- ______ →
- ______ →

STEP 4:
VALUE BEHAVIORS

- ______
- ______
- ______
- ______

STRATEGY

1 Know Your Professional Values

STEP 1: FIRST PASS

*Circle or mark the words that best describe your **PROFESSIONAL** values.*

- O Benefits
- O Brand I use and trust
- O Building/campus amenities
- O Culture I respect/trust
- O Entrepreneurial spirit
- O Equity stake
- O Expense account
- O Fast, nimble culture
- O Flexibility
- O Global brand
- O Income
- O Inclusive/diverse
- O International assignments
- O Launching pad
- O Leader I respect/trust
- O Location
- O Mission-driven
- O Opportunity for learning and development
- O Pension/retirement
- O Prestige of association
- O Product/service I believe in
- O Proximity to family
- O Public/government/foreign service
- O Resource-rich environment
- O Risk-taking culture
- O Safety
- O Security
- O Skill/development potential
- O Stock options
- O Team atmosphere
- O Tenure
- O Title
- O Travel
- O Union
- O Upward mobility
- O Wellness initiatives
- O Work from home
- O Work-life balance
- O Workspace (air quality, natural light, temperature, acoustics)
- O ____________
- O ____________
- O ____________

Don't see a word you like? Fill in your own.

Take your time. It may take hours, days, even weeks to decide. This isn't a shopping list you rush to make before a trip to the store.

STEP 2:
SHORT LIST

Choose your favorite values from step 1 and list them below.

- ____________________
- ____________________
- ____________________
- ____________________
- ____________________

STEP 3:
MY PROFESSIONAL VALUES

Tighten your list even more to finalize your values, and write them below.

- ____________________
- ____________________
- ____________________

This is a narrowing process to help you finalize your personal values.

STEP 4:
VALUE BEHAVIORS

Describe what your values look like in your behaviors.

- ____________________
- ____________________
- ____________________

STRATEGY 1

Know Your Professional Values

BUILD YOUR *PERSONAL* ACRONYM

Write your values in hierarchal order on the lines below and place the first letter of each in the respective box to the left to build your acronym.

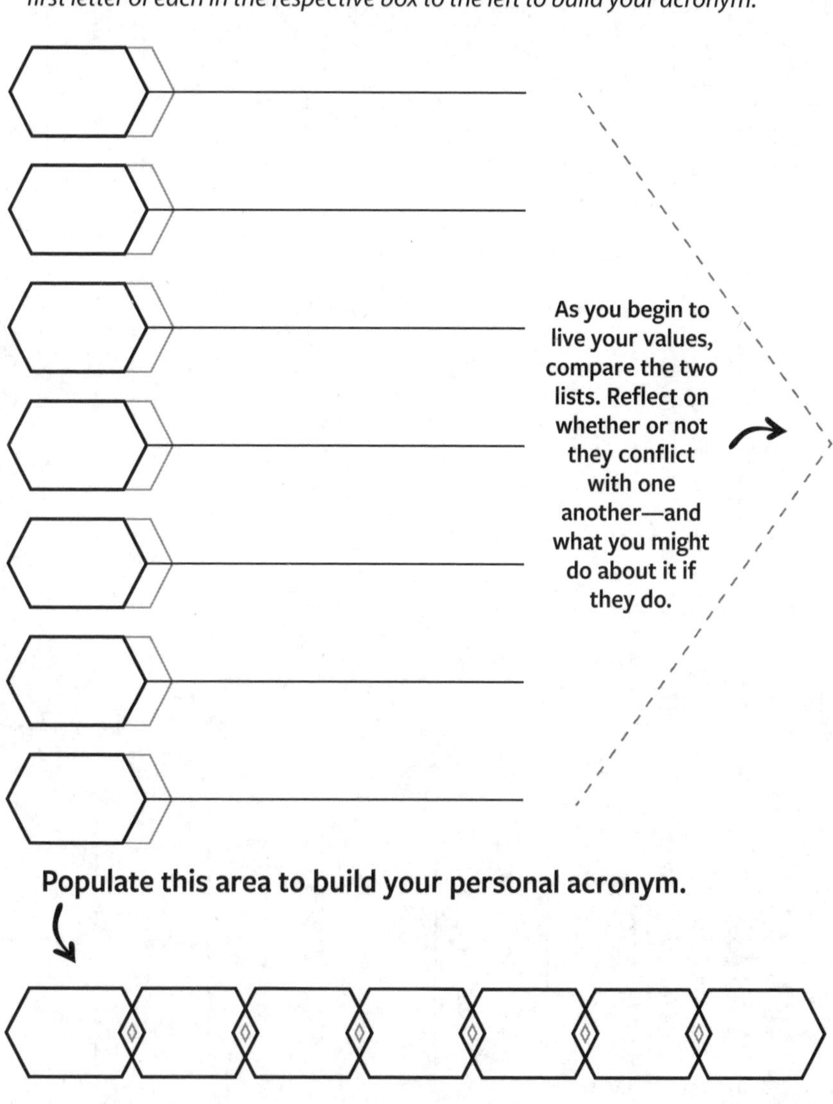

BUILD YOUR *PROFESSIONAL* ACRONYM

Write your values in hierarchal order on the lines below and place the first letter of each in the respective box to the right to build your acronym.

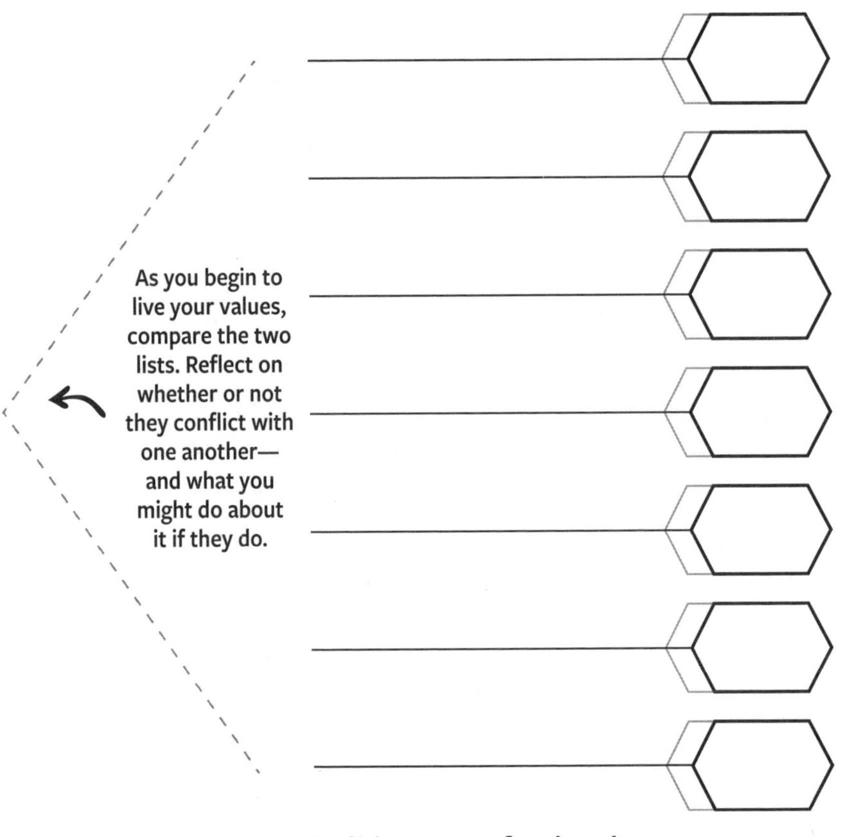

Populate this area to build your professional acronym.

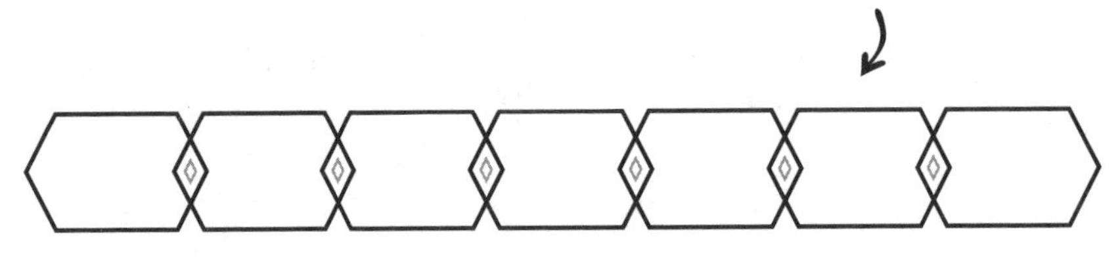

STRATEGY

2

Decide If You're a Specialist or a Generalist

Opening disclaimer: truth be told, I really created this strategy for those of you who identify as a Generalist, like me. You may have an education or set of experiences that are broad in nature, unlike others in your life who have an annoying level of clarity about what their career is going to look like. This chapter is the gift I'm giving you that I wish someone had handed me thirty-plus years ago.

The early years of my career, although very successful in their own right, are a textbook example of what I think describes a Generalist—and the ensuing struggle, confusion, conflict, anxiety, and even paralysis that follow many of us experiencing uncertainty in our professional calling. This often results in Generalists comparing ourselves to Specialists, who seem to have a remarkable sense of clarity and confidence about their skills and career direction. My hope is that, regardless of whether you identify as a Generalist or a Specialist, you can gain some insight and even liberation to explore your own intentionality free from the comparison of others.

This comparison happens so often there's even a name for it: the comparison conundrum. It's a concept with which I'm intimately acquainted. In fact, I've written about it in nearly all my preceding books.

The comparison conundrum is a long thread running through all my work. Perhaps in part because it motivates some, plagues others, and, for the rest of us, likely does both. The comparison conundrum proposes that almost every facet of our lives is based in our comparison to other people.

It's a tricky thing, isn't it? Finding the balance between comparing ourselves to others and having it deflate us or, better, marshaling that comparison toward our motivation to achieve our self-determined goals. For those who believe they *don't* compare themselves with others, I'd suggest you're probably in denial. It's absolutely happening, consciously and subconsciously.

Comparison to others starts early in life. As soon as we're born, we're compared to our siblings and parents: "Oh, he looks just like his brothers." "She's smaller than her sister, isn't she?" "Wow, he looks just like Cousin Pete, but he has his mother's eyes." Then, from preschool to elementary school, we're compared to our peers in nearly every category, from our manual dexterity to our weight and height. Every parent, including me, seems fixated on how their children measure up, literally and metaphorically, to their friends' children.

It only becomes more intense as we enter high school and college. Our mental focus, emotional regulation, athletic ability, academic success, social popularity, and more are up for comparison against everyone else's. And it doesn't stop when school is over—the essence of every professional raise and promotion is commonly determined by how we stack up against our peers. Raises, bonuses, stock options, equity . . . it's all part of the comparison conundrum. And since it's impossible to escape, learning how to deal with it is increasingly a life skill and a "sur-thrive-al" competency.

As I reflect on my own childhood, I see I was raised in a life of comparison, not as an implicit strategy from my parents but more as the consequence of being the only sibling of a superstar older brother, Mike. With four years between us, we were distant emotionally, mostly because we were always physically in different schools. Honestly, I never knew the guy until I was in my midthirties and we were both professionally established.

In many families, the oldest child is often the model for those who follow. Research on birth order has demonstrated that the firstborn is often a compliant rule follower who craves approval and is likely an overachiever.[1] That's certainly proven true with my own three sons and in my wife's family as well. Too often, the oldest child is viewed as the standard for all who follow. There's huge pressure on them, eclipsed only by the pressure on those down the line who are trying to live up to that established expectation.

Today, Mike is one of my best friends, and I hope he feels the same about me. But try following an honor-roll student, a star tennis player, and a guy who academically scholarshipped his way into college. I don't think my community college offered any scholarships or taught me that *scholarshipped* wasn't a real word. Then, to put a cherry on his engineering degree, after a few years working for several Fortune 50 companies, Mike received a full scholarship to MIT, where he earned a master's degree in business process before going on to become a Six Sigma Master Black Belt expert and serve as the CEO of two Amazon-owned companies. Hello, therapy.

Hey, Big Pharma, how about some R&D aimed at developing a pill for the comparison conundrum? I can already hear the commercial disclaimer: "Some patients taking Comparus experience side effects including stronger than expected confidence, higher self-esteem, upward mobility in their careers, and all-around improved relationships."

Okay, so I won't be a copywriter for Big Pharma. Let's return to the full package that was my brother.

The shadow was large, people.

I was swallowed up by it, and not so much because I wasn't achieving the accolades Mike was but more because I felt that what I accomplished never seemed like enough or was never even valued in the eyes of our parents. In large part that's because they appeared to relate and identify with Mike's chosen career path, which was safe, predictable, and understandable. Unlike mine. Not to say I was a slouch. I managed to become the high school student body president, and I worked and traveled in positions on US congressional and presidential campaigns. I led twenty employees at a local hot-spot restaurant with a side hustle as a realtor, the youngest in central Florida at the time, and even managed to sell some six-figure properties while still in my teens! But because it all seemed unrelatable to the well-prescribed path my parents equated with success, I sensed none of it was valued, and I felt discouraged.

If an occupation didn't bestow a recognizable "badge," my parents didn't seem to understand it and therefore didn't seem to value it. Careers that came with a designation such as *engineer*, *teacher*, *lawyer*, or *dentist* were seen as valid and valuable. I'm guessing even *taxi driver* would've been preferable to the nebulous domains of sales or marketing or that even more ethereal pursuit called "thought leadership" that I excel in now as an author, podcast host, and keynote speaker.

To this day, my mother would be hard pressed to define exactly how I earn a living. She and my father have been forgiven, as I eventually let go of the need for their validation once I realized that for them it appeared to be all about the badge. As I came to learn more about my parents' upbringing, I better understood their perceived obsession with security, as both were raised in homes without the safety or stability such a "badge" career provides.

Of course, in life our feelings and opinions aren't always based in fact, but our experiences do become our frame of reference and are deeply inculcated in our memories.

It wasn't until I interviewed David Epstein during an episode of the *On Leadership with Scott Miller* podcast that I finally understood how deeply buried I'd been in the comparison conundrum in our small family dynamic, not to mention the emotional toll it had taken on my self-esteem and confidence. Reading David's bestselling book *Range: Why Generalists Triumph in a Specialized World* and absorbing our subsequent interview was perhaps the most liberating event of my own professional life. I realized, decades later than I would have liked, that I was a Generalist comparing myself to my Specialist brother.

The Generalist Versus the Specialist

A Generalist is typically "knowledgeable about many topics and has various interests, skills and hobbies" while a

Specialist is "someone who is an expert in a certain field of study, occupation or practice."[2] Most of us fall into one of these two very different camps. Specialists often know early in life—during their college endeavors or even sooner—that they intend to pursue a particular passion or career such as veterinary medicine, aviation, military service, cosmetology, or architecture. We all had those friends in high school who selected potential colleges based on the strength of their journalism or premed programs. I marveled at these classmates (and of course by "marveled at" I mean "hated"). Some people have that unique talent, calling, voice, passion, vision, and direction around their careers unnaturally early in life. With this early clarity comes the upside of momentum toward that goal. It's something most Specialists can relate to.

And, as with most things in life, I think there's a downside to such clarity as well. I have a friend who's an OB-GYN, and I assume she can't easily envision pivoting from that. At least not too far. After ten years of schooling and hundreds of thousands of dollars invested in her career, she's essentially placed her bets on female health, and she's all in. A pivot beyond medical care must seem both unrealistic and even irresponsible at this point.

This friend has delivered thousands of babies, and as you would expect, that might burn a person out. After nearly two decades of such work, she needed a break. Unless you have friends willing to share some of the downsides of working in the medical profession, it can all seem awesome as they pull up to the hospital in their Range Rovers. But the grind is real, and my friend was feeling it. She transitioned into working as a hospitalist and then another administrative role, but finally settled on a practice more focused on women's holistic health needs. This is a great example of a Specialist practicing a pivot that isn't totally outside their realm. I don't know many ophthalmologists who become federal judges or real estate appraisers. I think such significant pivots are rare.

There are vast benefits to being a Specialist, and I think one of them is likely not suffering from comparison conundrum—at least not as much as most Generalists do. I could be wrong, but I doubt many chemical engineers making $96,000 a year right after graduating from college are thinking, *You know, I wish I'd pursued a communications degree so I could be working in a PR firm and making $22 an hour hosting a local event so my "creator" client can build an online following in the hopes of somehow monetizing it all.*

THAT NEVER HAPPENS. It's always the other way around. *Good grief, I just graduated from college, have $130,000 in student loans, and I'm working for $22 an hour? How did my friend have the clarity and skills to pursue a path that landed her as an engineer at Chevron where she's crushing it—and they're offering to pay for her MBA, plus she gets a paid sabbatical after her sixth year?! Plus beer on tap after 4 p.m. . . .*

Yeah, I hated those kinds of friends.

To the Generalists

Welcome to my world, fellow Generalists—a category that represents a vast population of professionals who hopscotch across jobs, roles, and industries. And who can relate, much more than Specialists can, to the comparison conundrum as they struggle more with focus early in their careers. Perhaps they love the flexibility and freedom of learning very different skills while satisfying their curiosity. Sounds like a good cover, but I don't think that's it. Generalists just happen, more often than not, to be late bloomers in terms of career focus and expertise. They don't know exactly what they want to do or are horrified at the thought of being pinned down and performing the same task every day. In many ways, spine surgeons aren't that much different from auto assembly line workers—they're paid much better, but their variability in work is similarly narrow.

In *Range*, David Epstein argues that it's the Generalists and not the Specialists who are primed to excel in a new economy. And while it may take Generalists longer to find their way in life, they can be more creative, make more connections, and have a breadth of experience and interests that position them to drive innovation.[3]

I wish I had a mentor who knew this and had pulled me aside early in my career to say, "Scott, it's going to be okay to be a Generalist. Keep learning. Keep growing. Build your skills. Collect as many mini badges as you can in your twenties, thirties, and beyond. You're going to learn a lot, about a lot, and then it will pop for you. All that knowledge will come together—the time you spent creating products, in research and development, and face-to-face with clients winning and losing deals. This will all pay off for you. Likely in leadership. These are the exact skills a CEO, COO, or CRO (chief revenue officer) needs. All the interviewing, hiring, and firing will work to your advantage. All the months you spent meeting and missing your revenue goals and making and missing your P&L projections, and all the client negotiations and presentations—they're going to come together masterfully for you as a Generalist. So embrace it all and enjoy the journey. Be patient. It *will* pay off, maybe just later than you'd like—and certainly later than for your Specialist nemesis."

My advice to you, fellow Generalists, is to have faith. But also have a plan. I hope you're both buoyed and sobered a bit at the prospect of what lies ahead, as I know many who have bounced around jobs, industries, and employers and were never able to stitch it all together in a culminating career.

This is the vital lesson: if you're a Generalist and don't synthesize all your experience at some point, you're simply an episodic, career-bouncing opportunist. And that's okay, if that works for you. But if that's not okay with you, recognize no one is going to knit everything together for you—you have to do this yourself, and you have to know when. I can't prescribe exactly how you will do this, as it's different for every Generalist, but the point is it's your responsibility to pull it together at some culminating point in your career and leverage it toward a set of marketable skills in an ever-changing marketplace. For me, this happened in my late forties, which is the same time I began to maximize my income toward the pinnacle of my career. Some refer to this as "talent stacking." Just be careful that all that stacking ultimately leads to the "badge" that works for you.

I doubt your preferences are going to pay off very well if you don't build a plan for how all your learning opportunities will prepare you for the culmination you're due. Thus, Strategy 4 is dedicated to your long-term plan. This is where you get to synthesize all your career insights into a cogent, multidecade plan that prevents you from picking up great skills along your wandering path but never integrating and leveraging them at the height of your career. Had I known all those skills I was learning along the way would eventually pay off, I would've certainly been less anxious and less frustrated with myself in my twenties, thirties, and early forties—and most importantly, not been mired in the envy, jealousy, and confusion that can come in the whirlpool of the comparison conundrum.

To the Specialists

Now, to those of you who identify as Specialists, congratulations. Truly, you somehow possessed a sense of clarity early in life that Generalists didn't—or didn't want to. Maybe it was a passion your parents validated or an interest a teacher ignited. Or maybe it was some other set of circumstances you're lucky to have fallen into. Or, for some, maybe it was a curse. Your sense of obligation led you into the family business because there were some generational expectations, and you felt a sense of duty to fulfill them. I've always marveled at my courageous friends whose parents owned successful businesses and were all set to inherit them but said, "No, thanks."

But none of this is to say Specialists can't become Generalists or Generalists can't become Specialists. Or that there aren't Generalists within Specialist categories. Current research shows that most Generalists will have between ten and twenty microcareers before they end their professional journeys, so if that's you, make them count. As a Specialist, stitch your own microcareers together (likely much fewer than the Generalist's), and be sure to invest the time into the exercises in Strategy 4 to think long-term, which is increasingly challenging in a short-term world.

············ EXERCISE SETUP ············

Decide If You're a Specialist or a Generalist

I don't suggest that being either a Specialist or Generalist is good or bad, right or wrong. It's more about which designation best describes you in your current career and how you can benefit from leveraging that awareness. Just as there are clear benefits to both, there are downsides as well. It all depends on your desire to become more intentional and deliberate about your career journey.

I suspect some of you will sense that being a Specialist might provide more security and certainty, while being a Generalist might offer more variety and flexibility. Conversely, others might see that Specialists are less likely or able to pivot to an entirely new career and might be "stuck," while Generalists might be stricken with a level of envy at the confidence and deliberateness that can come from being a Specialist. Keep in mind that your path might migrate from Specialist to Generalist, or vice versa, at some point in your career. Don't become frustrated and stagnant because you're trapped in the comparison conundrum, benchmarking your path and success against someone else's. It's a dangerous trap we can all fall into.

You'll notice the following exercise is more about introspection than action. It's designed to build awareness of your current state so you can more deliberately decide your future state and release any desire to compare yourself to anyone else.

Decide If You're a Specialist or a Generalist

SPECIALIST ROLES	VS	GENERALIST ROLES
Security & Certainty		*Variety & Flexibility*

SPECIALIST ROLES

- Accountant/CPA
- Actuary
- Applied Mathematician
- Automotive/Machine Technician
- Chemist
- Conservationist
- Engineer (Chemical, Electrical, Aerospace, etc.)
- Environmental Scientist
- Educator/Professor
- Forensic Scientist
- Hydrologist
- IT Specialist (e.g., Computer-Network Architect)
- Microbiologist
- Military Specialist
- Nurse
- Pharmacist
- Physician/Surgeon
- Pilot
- Software Specialist
- Specialized Consultant (e.g., Retail Strategy)
- Statistician
- Veterinarian

GENERALIST ROLES

- Business Management
- Communications
- Copywriter
- Entrepreneur
- Event Coordinator
- Financial Modeler
- General Consultant (Management, Sales, etc.)
- Hospitality
- HR Generalist
- IT Generalist (Support Tech, Web Designer, etc.)
- Marketing
- Operations
- Product Development
- Product Management
- Project Management
- Public Relations
- Research Analyst
- Sales
- Social Media Manager
- Social Worker
- Software Generalist
- Travel Agent

There is no right or wrong to being a specialist or a generalist. Also remember, it's never too late to change.

QUESTIONS TO PONDER

Given my talents, skills, education and interests, which designation do I most naturally gravitate to—Generalist or Specialist—and what is my comfort level with that designation?

Given my chosen designation:

What fears does the designation create or minimize in me?

What passions does the designation ignite in me?

What are the potential benefits of my designation?

What are the potential risks of my designation?

How do these insights inform or instruct my journey as I build my multidecade long-term plan in Strategy 4 and move from an accidental to an intentional career?

STRATEGY

3

Study Yourself

I recently interviewed a Fortune 500 CEO for the *C-Suite Conversations with Scott Miller* podcast. He led several apparel companies, and I asked him, "What are the common skills you're looking for in all new hires?"

"Hands down, EQ," he responded. "Specifically, the ability to read the body language and emotions of others."

That was one of the most succinct responses I'd heard after asking the same question to over a hundred C-suite guests, but they all pretty much said the same thing—they seek out emotionally mature people to hire. It reminds me of another interview with author Patty McCord, who served as the chief talent officer for Netflix. When I asked her a similar question, she put it this way: "At Netflix, we did our best to hire fully formed adults." Then she went on to share that it was pretty much impossible, as we're always growing in maturity, but her point was the same—our ability to relate and get along well with others is a skill we never really master.

The popular social scientist Eric Barker, who wrote the books *Barking Up the Wrong Tree* and *Plays Well with Others*, was another podcast interviewee who doubled down on this sentiment. Okay, maybe "Plays well with others" sounds like a line your teacher checked (or in my case likely didn't) on your first-grade report card. But what a superb skill to put on the top of your résumé or LinkedIn profile:

> Scott Jeffrey Miller
> Open to Opportunities.
> Strategic Thinker. Creator of Systems and Processes. Profit Focused. Excellent Communicator. Plays Well with Others.

I wonder what the SEO (search engine optimization) looks like for recruiters searching for candidates who play well with others. Probably OFF THE CHARTS. But therein also lies the problem. We all know we need to get along with others to get stuff done, but we can be so focused on understanding other people's personalities, nuances, failings, body language, emotional cues, and quirks that we don't spend enough time understanding our own. When was the last time you asked yourself, *How easy is it to get along with me, and what do other people need to do differently to accommodate my personality that I refuse to acknowledge or change?* This chapter is all about gaining self-awareness of what it's like to be in any type of relationship with you, personal or professional.

A Quick Exercise

I'm now inviting you to complete two exercises with a short, highly scientific test at the end that comes with instant scoring. None of this "the professor takes a week to grade your paper." You get to learn your score instantly.

Quickly think of ten people you work with or in some way interact with in your life. Not only your friends or family but professional colleagues too. I want you to write their name in the left column and then, in the next two columns, write one word about them that's a compliment and one that's a criticism. If there's any chance someone else could see these pages, don't write out their name and instead use a letter to identify them.

NAME	COMPLIMENT	CRITICISM

Pretty easy, wasn't it? Especially that last column. We generally have a top-of-mind awareness of other people's faults and interpersonal issues.

Now repeat the exercise, but this time from *their* perspective. What do they likely think about you? Keep their name (or letter) in the left column but write a compliment you think they would give you, then a criticism—the harsher the better.

NAME	COMPLIMENT	CRITICISM

NAME	COMPLIMENT	CRITICISM

Here's the scoring process:

Fail = I had no issue immediately identifying criticisms about ten people I know but really struggled to think of serious, legitimate criticisms they might have of me.

Pass = I had no issue immediately identifying criticisms about ten people I know and also needed more lines to write detailed criticisms they likely have about me.

That's it, pass or fail. And you should also get the point: it's a lot easier putting other people under the microscope than ourselves. But let's rectify that now, as it's an essential part for your intentional career journey.

Introspection Should Lead to Change

Studying yourself is as aspirational, valuable, and relevant today as when the Greeks first carved "Know thyself" on the temple of Apollo. Centuries later, a version of this aphorism can be found at the wildly less popular tabernacle of Scott, where the words "You're annoying to others—figure out why and fix it" have been dutifully inscribed.

Yes, introspection is a difficult ask. But we're not meant to stop there. It comes with an invitation to change. And let's face it, change is hard. Adding to the complexity is the fact we've been conditioned to focus our attention on everyone else and not ourselves. Studying and learning from others can certainly be a vital part of our personal, professional, and career development. But when such exploration is completely outward-focused, we miss the opportunity for greater self-awareness and a sense of how others view us in return.

Consider this: if a group of researchers were to follow you around for a week, read all your emails and social posts, listen in on your meetings and conversations, and watch where you go and what you do, what would they discover? And what if they expanded their research by examining your broader life, reviewing your high school and college transcripts, and interviewing your teachers, neighbors, friends, former romantic partners, or anyone in any kind of relationship with you? If they had access to your credit score, human resource files, bank accounts, and other legal documents, what conclusions would they come to?

Would you be labeled as an energy infuser or drainer? Would they determine that you try to lift others up or find opportunities to tear them down? Would they resolve that you tend to own up to your mistakes and apologize sincerely or dig in deeper and grow more defensive? Would they find that you take delight in the success of others and view your relationships through an abundance mindset? Or do you operate through a scarcity paradigm, doing what it takes to ensure you win no matter the cost?

This idea of studying ourselves is a bit counterintuitive. After all, we buy books, listen to podcasts, attend speeches, and watch interviews to glean important information from the experts. And this is absolutely a wise investment of our time. Want to be a great marketer? Study Seth Godin. Want to build better relationships? Study Brené Brown. Want to write a book? Study Adam Grant, Liz Wiseman, or James Clear. Want to live a more balanced life? Study Arianna Huffington. No doubt some of our greatest insights can come from studying the behavior, success, and setbacks of others.

But studying others is only part of the equation when it comes to getting and keeping your career on course. You have to become a master of yourself. Thus, this chapter is about self-awareness, not *other*-awareness. Such a focus matters because you're definitely not as self-aware as you think you are. I know, you're thinking, *But I'm the exception, Scott. I reflect on my life and goals all the time. I work on self-improvement and consistently strive to get better. So while I'm sure this is good advice for practically everyone else, I've got this one handled.*

News flash: you don't.

Yep, everyone thinks that (1) They're more self-aware than they are, and (2) Their current level of awareness is sufficient.

Nope!

Your lack of self-awareness is the reason you were demoted, let go, laid off, or passed over for that promotion. It's the cause behind most of your strained relationships. It's at the root of your interpersonal failures and why you're falling short of your goals, failing to adapt to change, and living your life through a rearview mirror and wallowing in regret. It's the largest reason you have conflict. As Dr. Covey was known for saying, "As long as you think the problem is out there, that very thought is the problem."

Understand How Others Experience You

To craft an intentional career requires you to develop a burning desire to understand how others experience being in a relationship with you—working with you, cooperating with you, teaming up with you, debating with you, leading you, or being led by you. You must become introspective and thoughtful as you look deeper into what's driving your actions and uncover the motives, intentions, biases, assumptions, emotions, and personality traits that fuel your behavioral engine. Learning to study yourself in this way can be the single most powerful habit you learn, manifesting the greatest number of benefits in your life.

But it's hard work.

It's also the reason I featured Tasha Eurich in a previous book *Master Mentors Volume 2: 30 Transformative Insights from Our Greatest Minds*. I consider her book *Insight* to be the best book ever authored about self-awareness. I also interviewed her on episode 131 of *On Leadership with Scott Miller*, and it's definitely a must-watch and must-listen conversation (yes, the podcast is video and audio).

Reflect for a moment: How much time in life have you spent actively, intentionally, and objectively studying yourself? This includes taking a hard look at the way you speak, argue, negotiate, collaborate, forgive, apologize, listen, grieve, and even celebrate. Have you really considered how you prioritize and get stuff done? Why you may be overly distracted or hyperfocused? Why or when you're happy or irate? Who you like and why? Where and when you're most fulfilled or frustrated?

Consider how those around you would answer these questions when asked about you. How would they describe what it's like to sit around a conference table with you during an in-person meeting? Or be with you through a multiday team strategy session? A Zoom or Teams call? How would they describe the experience of cohabitating a ten-by-ten trade show booth with you for three days? To be assigned to collaborate on a project with you?

Honestly investigating any one of these can dramatically improve your self-awareness. Thankfully, you can do more than guess what it's like to be around you. A key part of studying yourself is asking for and digesting feedback from others, or what I call your Team of Eight, which I will address later in this chapter.

A popular aphorism declares, "The most important relationship you will ever have is with yourself." This is profound, when you think about it. It means you're willing to pay the price to understand not only the *way* you act but *why* you tend to do so. Let's face it, your personality is the way it is for a reason. It drives how you think, speak, respond, listen, and interact with others, and it's at the heart of everything you feel and how you behave. Now, admittedly, attempting such personal analysis may be an exercise best accomplished between you and your therapist or coach. But even so, I believe you can muster sufficient courage to look objectively inward, develop new skills, and nudge yourself (at the very least) toward the version of you whom *you* most want to be. Let me offer three work examples; consider if there's any "you" in these experiences.

Case Study: The Most Talented and the Most Despised

Several years ago, I was leading a team of about forty associates. I'd individually selected every member, so their ultimate performance and the overall culture of the division was very much a reflection on my leadership capabilities. I'd inherited no one and grew this team from the ground up, so there was nobody else to blame when performance lagged or interpersonal issues arose. Of course, talented people have squabbles and disagreements—that can be a sign that opinions are being shared openly and there's freedom to dissent. But overall, a team's culture is defined by how most people behave most of the time. There can be outliers, of course, and these can have a disproportionate impact on overall culture and performance. We've all seen this happen as a single person becomes a cancer that's brutal to engagement, retention, and productivity.

Back to my team. I'd assembled a superb group of achievers who generally worked well with each other and surfaced issues easily so they could be addressed and resolved. We'd grown from a small team of five to peaking at about forty as we brought in other divisions from the company. Naturally, with such growth, the culture and vibe changed. One team member, who was unquestionably creative and competent in their field of expertise, was also a train wreck interpersonally. The team initially forgave this as we didn't have time to nitpick the small but annoying behaviors that began to surface. We were crucial to the company's successes and moved so quickly from project to project that I believed a change in their employment was a nonstarter. (I am certain I was also frequently on the receiving end of that team's generosity and pre-forgiveness, so to those members reading this, thank you for your patience and loyalty.)

Said another way, this team member had zero context for how difficult they made it to work with them, even though over the course of many years I'd surfaced the topic with them, albeit perhaps too superficially. After a while, it reached the point where I had to intervene as the leader. Their lack of self-awareness threatened to unravel the necessary working cohesion of the team. So I sat them down and made the severity of the situation clear in the most straightforward, no niceties, change-your-behavior-or-you're-out kind of way. They calmly listened, then with some emotion professed to be surprised at the feedback and lamented that nobody had ever told them before. That certainly wasn't absolutely true, but in retrospect I'd never had a true "change or you're out" intervention with them.

After this emotional conversation, where I professed my support but also my commitment to end their employment if immediate changes weren't made, they agreed to work with a coach I'd identified and made available. Which is where you'd expect a positive ending to the story, right? Only it didn't turn out that way. In the following weeks they complained about every aspect of the coaching engagement. Blaming. Obfuscating. Making excuses.

Frustrated beyond belief, I was done.

Now, to clarify, this person remains one of the most talented associates I've ever worked with. They truly brought their A game to every initiative with enormous creativity and attention to detail. They genuinely cared about the success of a project and the result. My experience with them consistently reinforced that they were trustworthy to deliver the highest quality work on time and had a relentless work ethic. I really wanted to like this person. But working with them was emotionally fatiguing because they were a cultural cancer on the team. They were fundamentally unlikable because of how incredibly difficult they were to work with. Ironically, if ballots were cast, my team would have voted this person a winner in two categories: most talented and most deserving of being kicked off the team.

Eventually this person and the team parted ways, and I wish them all success on their continued process of building their own self-awareness. That's something we should all be continually working on. Our blind spots can ultimately sink us if not addressed.

Case Study: From Uninvited to Disengaged

Another former colleague of mine was also supremely talented but interpersonally challenging. One day this person, who reported to me, complained that they found themselves increasingly isolated from many divisions in the company and, as a function of their role, they needed to be better connected and involved in more meetings and conversations so they could properly execute their responsibilities. Although they reported to me in one division, they had a cross-functional role and felt in the dark on many vital topics. The truth was this person had a valid reason for being included in many meetings that they were simply not being invited to. When they approached me about the issue, their exact words were, "I need to be involved in these conversations. I don't understand why I'm not being invited to these meetings."

Drawing on the courage required by all people leaders and the lessons I'd learned from the prior colleague about being direct, I responded gently but clearly. "I know why you're not being invited to these meetings. Would you like my insight?"

"Yes," they said enthusiastically.

I then described in clear and painful detail what it was like joining any setting where they were included. "The reason is you demonstrate an inability to stay on topic. Repeatedly. You take team members down rabbit holes and meandering labyrinths, which someone actually once described to me as your 'crazy trains to nowhere.'"

From the person's reaction, this was obviously *not* what they were expecting to hear. So I continued by citing specific instances, times, places, dates, and other demonstrable facts. I was mindful not to crush their self-esteem in offering this feedback, but I felt they needed to hear that when a meeting was scheduled and their name was proposed as a participant, without fail someone would ask, "Okay, but *should* we invite them?" And if they could find a way to hold the meeting without this person, they would do so.

Rationale for the uninvites included sentiments like, "It will just be too difficult. . . . We will never stay on topic. . . . Bringing them into the meeting will absolutely ensure it goes sideways." Even though teams in the organization liked this individual personally, the consensus was that their levels of focus, discipline, and self-awareness were so low they couldn't be allowed to jeopardize the meeting time.

Ouch. Double ouch.

Every word I told them in our candid conversation was true. And this person needed to hear it to have any chance of salvaging their brand, credibility, and ultimately their job. Unfortunately, instead of becoming more self-aware and contributing in a way that kept meetings on track and focused, they shut down completely. They were offended and hurt, so they disengaged and largely refused to comment or even speak a word in future meetings. In essence, they swung the pendulum of their behavior to the opposite side, which was uncomfortably noticeable to everyone around them.

This was obviously not a wise strategy, and I sat them down again and explained this during our next one-on-one. I coached that they needed to find a reasonable balance and suggested they identify a "meeting buddy" and ask this person to text them, send a private message, or offer up some signal when they were off track or "going too far" on any specific topic.

Incidentally, I do the same thing. With some frequency, when I'm on a Zoom or Teams meeting and sense I might be off topic or pressing a subject too harshly, I'll text someone I respect in the meeting and ask them if they think I should pull back or if I'm talking too much.

Case Study: Jack of All Trades, Master of None

I've worked with a slew of very talented individuals, including many with Ivy League educations and Fortune 50 backgrounds. One individual had neither but certainly presented themselves as such. Not untruths, just an assumed level of expertise on *everything* that made them interpersonally fatiguing. They indeed had experience in operations, sales, marketing, and product development. This person could write, deliver presentations to large audiences, moderate, you name it. And with such a breadth of experience came a robust level of confidence. Confidence that unfortunately translated into arrogance. They had an "I'm right" persona that permeated nearly every engagement and left no opinion unexpressed. I don't think this was their real mindset, and if they had known this, I bet they'd be horrified. Then again, maybe not. I wasn't invested in them enough to have an intervention. Now, if they'd asked me, I'd have been happy to share, as I have courage in excess.

But I know many others viewed them similarly, and it absolutely became their brand. From the front line into the C-suite, people knew exactly what to brace themselves for when this person got involved: they were right and others were wrong. And the quicker others came to this understanding the less painful it would be. What's interesting is when you scratched below the surface, their ideas and solutions were pretty much the same for every problem.

What's that adage? "A master of everything is a master of none." And that described them perfectly.

Sadly.

This is what Liz Wiseman, in her book *Multipliers*, would term "the smartest person in the room." Always. And the one nobody wants to work with—and most certainly not for.

Now that we've moved through three real-world examples of the limiting effects of not being self-aware, you may have found elements of your own experiences in them, whether in dealing with others or in candid moments of honest self-reflection. Either way, you can build self-awareness as a skill through the practice of studying yourself. Let me offer two suggestions for what you can do as well as provide an exercise for building a trusted feedback team so you can learn from those around you.

Two Habits for Introspective Self-Study

Because self-awareness is a journey that requires dedication and commitment, it often involves moving outside of our comfort zones. Consider two practices that can help: mindful meditation and journaling.

Mindful Meditation

Mindful meditation is an ancient practice that has been gaining popularity in recent years as a powerful tool for self-awareness and personal growth. It can help you connect with your inner self and become more aware of your thoughts, feelings, and emotions without judgment or interference. By paying attention to internal experiences, you can gain deeper insight into your true intentions, motivations, and desires, which helps you make wiser decisions aligned with who you are rather than what outside forces might expect you to do. The practice can also help you identify patterns in your thinking you may not have been aware of before.

Journaling

Journaling can be another way to build increased self-awareness through self-study. Writing down your thoughts and experiences on a regular basis allows you to reflect on them from a different perspective and gain a better understanding of why you think and act the way you do. It can also help you track your progress as you work toward becoming more self-aware. If this isn't a habit for you, start by choosing the right journal and writing materials. Look for what feels inviting and has a pleasing aesthetic, and don't be afraid to try different styles or formats if something isn't working out.

Additionally, budget time each day for writing. This can be any time that works with your schedule, but aim for consistency; try setting aside the same time each day or week so that it becomes a regular part of your routine. If possible, dedicate a quiet space just for journaling where you won't be distracted or interrupted by outside activities and noise.

Finally, when beginning to write in your journal of choice, jot down simple things such as events that occurred during the day or how you feel about certain topics. It may take some practice before you find yourself able to reflect deeply on heavier topics or feelings, but with each passing entry it'll become easier and more natural. As you continue writing, pay attention to not only what you record but also how it affects your behavior, as this can provide valuable clues into why you think and act the way you do.

To help you deepen your self-reflection and begin to build self-awareness, try using these journaling prompts:

- Who are the people in my life who tend to generate an immediate negative response from me? Can I better identify what triggers me and show improved restraint in the future?
- What's my level of impulsivity, and do my immediate reactions cause me regret or embarrassment or minimize my influence? How could I set better personal boundaries to protect me from myself?
- What are some of what I perceive to be my key strengths that others might see as my key weaknesses? Self-confidence? Voice modulation? Eye contact? Decisiveness?
- What are some beliefs I'm holding on to because they provide me a level of security and protection, when in fact they may make me obsolete, rigid, or even scared?

Self-Study Through External Feedback—Your Team of Eight

In the accompanying exercise, I encourage you to build your "Team of Eight," individuals representing both your personal and professional life whom you trust to give you raw, actionable feedback on what it's like to be in a relationship with you.

Now, you can solicit loads of feedback from people, but if you're not in the mindset to receive, digest, and implement it, it's a useless exercise. Actually, it's worse than useless; it's damaging and diminishing to your relationships and reputation. The only thing worse for your brand than not asking for feedback is asking for it and then dismissing it, or pretending to accept it and then failing to act on it. This proves to the person giving feedback that you're not serious about growing and learning, and they'll feel used and manipulated. So you'll need to learn some skills on your path to increasing the flow of quality feedback coming your way.

Before we discuss those skills, let's talk about how unlikely people are to give true feedback. Truthfully, most people are cowards. This isn't a character flaw but rather a personality trait. When you ask someone in your social circle to give you feedback on what it's like to be your pickleball partner, or a member of the same book club, or serve on a committee together, most of the time they'll respond with, "Oh, you're great. I love how you . . ." which is probably *nonsense*. That's a total waste of your and their time. First, they have a trove of suggestions on how you could be a better secretary of the PTA or member of the HOA or whatever. But they aren't going to verbalize it. There's zero upside for them to do so and loads of downside. Rarely, if ever, has such a conversation ended with the person receiving the feedback announcing, "I'm so thankful to you for sharing all of that. I will treasure this conversation for years to come. Thank you for making that investment in me."

Nope. That won't happen. Ever!

Why? Because the receiver of that feedback is really thinking, *Well, how dare you. Are you kidding me? Do you know what it's like to work with you? How could you possibly think that?*

You get the point. When we receive criticism, our reflex is to become defensive and metaphorically crawl into the safety of our protective shell. So, if you want to build a thriving career and increase your self-awareness, you must make it safe for others to tell you their truth about how they see and experience you. And that means they need to understand and believe you truly want to know what it's like to be around you. Remember that soliciting, receiving, and processing feedback is entirely your responsibility, and only you can create the conditions where people feel both safe and vulnerable enough to tell you their truth.

Notice I said *their* truth and not *the* truth. Feedback is subjective and may not be accurate or factual. It's ultimately for you to decide its value and their motivation for sharing it with you. I've been on the receiving end of some brutal feedback about me that was completely accurate. I've also been on the receiving end of some brutal feedback that I deduced was completely misplaced because it was grounded in that person's jealousy of me or was a transference of their feelings about some other person who looks or acts like me (their former spouse, leader, friend, and so on).

Consider starting with the following words (or your natural version of them) as you begin to contemplate your Team of Eight and the exercise at the end of this chapter: "I'm currently building my self-awareness regarding what it's like to ________________ with me. I've been encouraged by a book I'm reading to find eight people in my life whose opinions I trust, and I've identified you as one of them. Would you be willing to talk with me about some specific behaviors I demonstrate that both delight and annoy you? Or, said another way, when you step back and look at my strengths and weaknesses (which we both know I have), what could I be doing more of or less of that you think could make me more effective in my role or life?"

Choose your Team of Eight carefully from both your personal life and your professional settings. You might need to give them time to think about the feedback they want to offer. Some might even prefer to send it via email or do it virtually. Most importantly, you want to demonstrate that you truly want and value anything they're willing to offer as you continue the journey of studying yourself. When one of your Team of Eight does offer some valuable and actionable feedback, validate it.

Consider your version of this statement: "Wow. That was so valuable to hear. I must admit it stings a bit, but let me tell you, genuinely, how much I value our relationship and friendship. I know this is an area I need to work on. If I'm vulnerable and honest, I've heard this before and have ignored it or outright denied it in the past. But you've convinced me it's an issue I need to address, and I know that wasn't easy for you. Thank you for taking the risk and telling me straight. I so value you."

Now, the exact verbiage of that statement may or may not align with how you talk, but you get the gist. Find a version that feels natural for you and the relationship. Then, when you receive actionable feedback, implement it and make a change. Because if a member of your Team of Eight takes the risk to move outside their comfort zone and talk straight with you, you must honor them by at least considering their feedback, so when they see changes in you, they'll become your unabashed defender and champion in the future.

EXERCISE SETUP

Study Yourself

This exercise can't be accomplished in one sitting, as studying yourself is a process, not an event. It requires you not only to be introspectively curious and mindful but also to continually solicit and receive feedback from others, which necessitates courage, patience, and humility.

1. Identify your Team of Eight from people you engage with frequently—ideally four from your personal life and four from your professional life. Don't just find people who love and adore you, as that's a waste of everyone's time. Choose people who may be annoyed by you or perhaps even dislike you. It's often such "detractors" who will teach you the most about yourself. Share with them that you recognize you've had differences in the past but would greatly appreciate their perspective as you genuinely attempt to study yourself and gain increased self-awareness.
2. Meet with each person separately—face-to-face, over the phone, on video conference, via email or text,

whichever way helps them feel at ease to give you courageous, actionable insights. Not everyone will be comfortable providing critical feedback, so be certain to create the right setting for each of them.

3. Ask each person:
    - What's one thing I do that annoys you?
    - What's one thing I do that delights you?
    - Could you further describe the impact my actions have had on you or others and what it has done to my "brand"? (Note: more on this topic in Strategy 5: Define and Build Your Brand.)

STRATEGY

3 Study Yourself

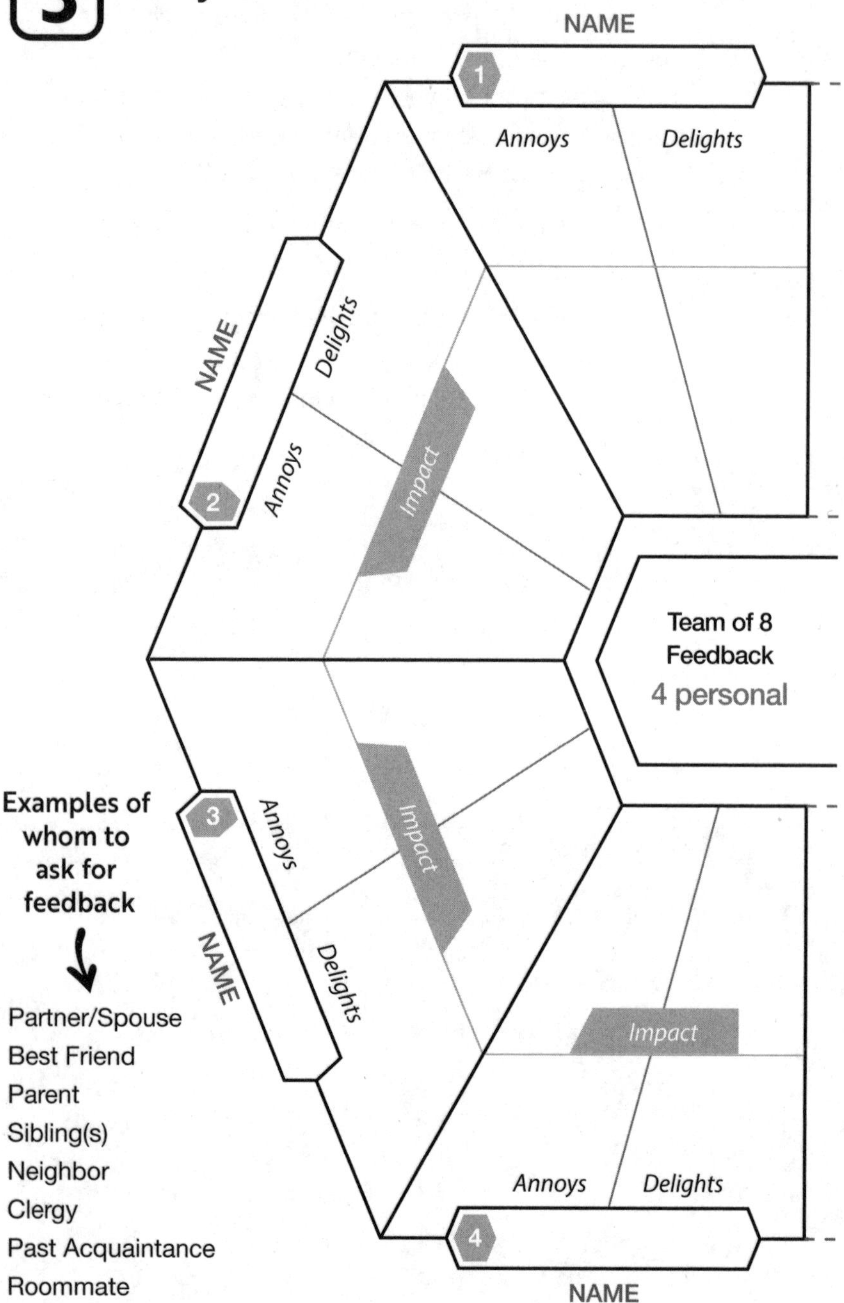

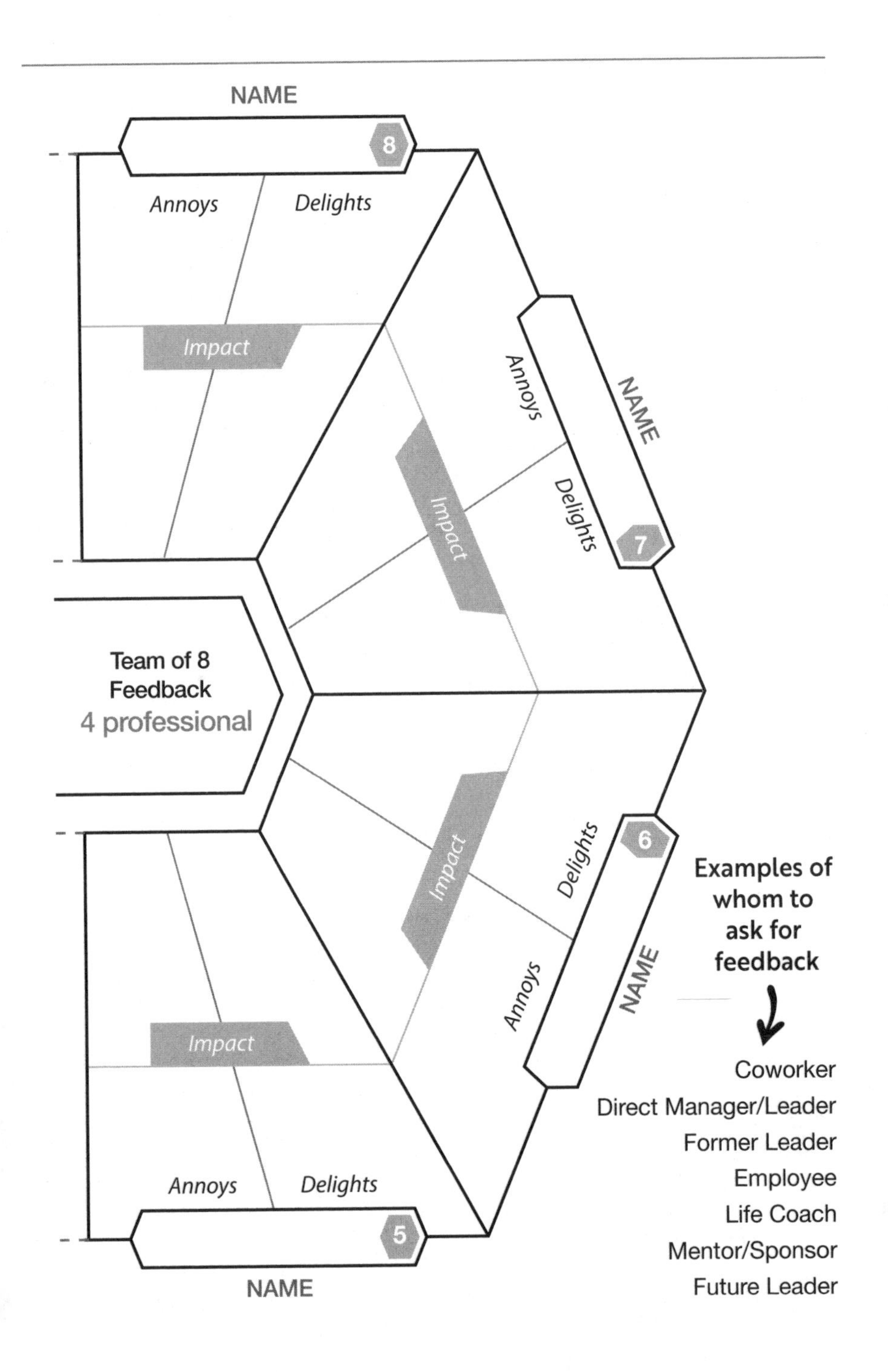
NAME
8
Annoys
Delights
Impact
Annoys
NAME
Delights
7
Impact
Team of 8
Feedback
4 professional
Delights
6
Impact
Annoys
NAME
Impact
Annoys
Delights
5
NAME
Examples of whom to ask for feedback
Coworker
Direct Manager/Leader
Former Leader
Employee
Life Coach
Mentor/Sponsor
Future Leader

STRATEGY 4

Illustrate and Recalibrate Your Long-Term Plan

Whenever I deliver a keynote at organizations and universities facilitating my Career on Course program, one of the most frequent questions I'm asked is, "What's the best decision you ever made in your career that enabled you to move from the front line to the C-suite quite swiftly?" The question beneath the question goes something like this: "Scott, how did you manage to keep your relevance and skills strong, maintain control over your professional life, and never become the victim of someone else's limiting view of your potential?" Chances are they wouldn't have worded it just like that, but that's the gist of it.

I give a two-part answer to this question: *flexibility* (to a lesser degree) and *long-term planning* (to a greater degree).

Flexibility

Much of my success came down to the fact that I was Gumby professionally, willing and able to do what most people weren't. For example, when I was in my midtwenties, I relocated across the country from Orlando to Salt Lake City (the cultural equivalent of moving to the moon for a single Catholic boy in his twenties), where I knew exactly one person. Then I moved to London, England, where I knew exactly no one (also a massive cultural change for a "go-go-gadget" American guy trying to find success in a more somber and reserved country). And then I moved back to Salt Lake City—on my way to Chicago, where I again knew no one. Followed by literally dozens of other courageous, risky, potentially dangerous bets I placed on myself throughout my career.

Not all of them worked out as planned, and I'm sure I sacrificed developing some deep relationships and even early romantic opportunities for the sake of my career. But as I look back, I wouldn't change anything, because this constant self-disruption instilled in me a level of self-confidence I otherwise never would've developed, as well as a set of professional skills that absolutely enabled me to follow a steep career trajectory that resulted in enough financial independence and stability to have some insulation from uncontrollable circumstances (downsizing, termination, and so forth).

I recognize that as a young and single professional I had more flexibility than if I'd had a family with children in school, parents with illnesses, or other reasons I needed to stay settled geographically. But you must decide for yourself what flexibility means given your unique set of circumstances, because they are crucial aspects of any intentional career.

Long-Term Planning

Besides my willing flexibility, the best decision I ever made as a young professional was to create a long-term plan, which is the core concept in Strategy 4. Then work that plan, year in and year out, decade after decade.

Sounds simple, yet few people have an actual career plan. Don't believe me? Go ahead and grab your well-constructed, often reviewed, and intentionally focused career plan and email a photograph of it to Scott@ScottJeffreyMiller.com so I can congratulate you. Oh wait . . . it doesn't exist? It's okay, you're not alone. And if you do happen to have one, great—I still have some valuable ideas to share with you in this chapter.

Let me take you back to when twenty-three-year-old me was living in Orlando. I worked for the Disney Development Company, the real estate development arm of the Walt Disney Company, known as the very front of the value chain for Disney. We built the theme parks, cruise ships, hotels, office buildings, and, in my case, the town of Celebration, which was a master-planned community and the future home of about twelve thousand people drawn to the Disney brand in central Florida. Disney hired me as a lowly college intern, and through a mix of skills and charm (more of the latter than the former), I turned a part-time college internship into a full-time, well-paid, salaried career that lasted four years and launched me into three decades of professional success.

The fateful evening happened in 1994. *The Lion King* reigned at the box office, a new sitcom called *Friends* debuted on NBC, and O.J. Simpson was about to make headlines with his infamous slow-speed chase. I was working full-time at Disney and going to school full-time in the evenings to finish my undergraduate degree. Yes, I worked at a forty-plus-hours professional job (coat and tie preferred) and then went to school four nights a week and all day Saturday. It sucked, but I left college virtually debt-free.

One evening (must have been a Friday, as I was in school every other night), I was having dinner alone at a TGI Fridays after work. I can still recall the exact table I sat at and what I ate. After I'd ordered and handed the menu to my server, I turned the paper placemat over and sketched out my four-decade career plan. Now, I'd never seen something like this done before—no one had inspired me or instructed me to do so. I'd simply read so much about the value of writing your goals down on paper, visualizing them, and then revisiting them that I began to do it for myself. I leveraged the knowledge I'd gained from my research and informal interviews with professors and professionals I worked with about organizational structures and the most successful career paths, and I went to work.

On the back of that placemat (which I still have in a box of precious life mementos), I sketched out my major career goals. I drew a long line from left to right and plotted where I was currently and where I wanted to be forty years later. Then I plotted important milestones as tick marks along the way. I did this by starting on the far right (this is vital) and then working my way back to the left.

The far right represented my ultimate career conquest. The far left represented my current role title, responsibilities, and level of compensation.

My scrawled plan became the best career decision of my life. It took thirty years for me to work my plan, while of course being open to some serendipitous opportunities along the way. But having a plan in hand, when nobody else around me did, put me well ahead of the need to compete with anyone other than myself.

Success Is Rarely Accidental

Careers that meander and are accidental are rarely a formula for success. Sure, outliers exist, and we hear the stories of wildly successful people who had no idea how they got where they did, and if not for this accident, or that rare leader, or just being in the right place at the right time, they would be in a very different situation. We tend to elevate such exceptions as the norm. But they are not. They make for great reading and entertaining interviews—unlike the person who envisioned a three-decade plan over dinner at TGI Fridays, worked it maniacally, and achieved their dream through self-disruption, flexibility, and a relentless work ethic. There's a reason the news offers up stories about lottery winners and not the four-decade professional plotter who becomes the self-made "millionaire next door" and ultimately has just as much freedom and flexibility.

As I foreshadowed in the introduction, my career stayed on course because I knew the course. I certainly hadn't traveled it in advance, but I'd studied it enough that I could draw the path forward. I knew where most of the obstacles would be, and I prepared for them. This is nothing new. The Apollo moon landing required an incredible amount of planning and preparation before venturing to a previously unvisited destination. Before the mission could materialize, the astronauts mapped out a precise course for their journey. The mission planners had to account for a variety of factors, from the effects of Earth's gravity on the trajectory of the spacecraft to ensuring they had enough fuel and supplies for the voyage and the return. NASA put together a team of experts who dedicated years of their time to drawing up a comprehensive road map.

While your career planning may not be as meticulous as a mission to the moon, it'd be a mistake to leave it up to the whims of chance. Or worse, the direction of someone else. You not only want to successfully launch your career off the platform; you want to arrive safely at your never-before-visited destination.

Now, I want to acknowledge a few emerging elephants in the room. For many of you reading this book, I'm of a different generation. At age fifty-five, I'm someone who was raised in a time where loyalty was the guiding force of most professional careers (and hence one of my core personal values). An ambition of nearly every professional, including many Specialists, was to create a stable career, ideally fulfilled at one organization.

I recognize that sentiment has vastly changed, and today the opposite can be true for many. Some professionals want to stay with a company for as short a time as possible. Not days, mind you, but as few years (or months) as it takes to learn new skills, get promoted a time or two, and master the industry enough to pivot up, across, or out. Which is often to the competition—something that, in my generation, would have made you a pariah, a turncoat, a traitor. Today it's not only commonplace, it's expected.

Additionally, the average tenure for most careers in one organization is about eighteen months—thirty-six at the most. As recently as five years ago, if I looked at your résumé and saw you had three careers in six years, I likely wouldn't have even interviewed you, thinking you were either a complete self-serving opportunist or worse, or you had the inability to thrive due to a lack of interpersonal skills, resulting in your constant jumping (or being pushed) from ship to ship. Now I would be the one hard-pressed to land a job anywhere, with twenty-eight years at one company on my résumé. Many (even you) might see me as inflexible, desperate, and likely too inculcated in "the way we always did it at X" to be nimble and agile enough to thrive in new and fast-changing environments. It's a sobering and true thought.

Career Rules Still Rely on Timeless Principles

Both of the previous examples are extremes, but you get my point: the rules may have changed, but the principles around an intentional career have not. What matters is you defining the career *you* want and then drawing on the values you outlined in Strategy 1 to chart your way forward. Security will be paramount for some, while for others it's not even a consideration. Some of you may see a very clear path to what your pinnacle is, while others don't want to be tied down to one linear course, finding value and even exhilaration in serendipity. For some of you, the day you're fired will be an invaluable gift, liberating you to find a new call to action. For others, being fired would be a nightmare because of the roles and responsibilities you have to people in your life. I see and validate all these circumstances as being relevant and important as you put your career on the course you choose. Your invitation is to take what's valuable to you and leave for others what isn't.

Understand Others' Paths and How Organizations Work

As I designed my long-term plan, I met with many professionals at various levels so I could understand what *their* paths looked like—where they started, what came next, and what was after that. I wanted to understand the setbacks, the lateral movements, and even the quantum leaps. Combined with illustrating an actual multiyear plan, this informal research with neighbors, community leaders, and mentors provided me an invaluable understanding of how organizations are actually structured.

When I came out of college, even with a few courses in organizational design, behavior, and communications, I was totally clueless how companies were organized. But after many conversations, I learned that most follow a general alignment around sales, marketing/communications, finance, operations, legal, R&D/innovation, product development, and human resources, each with varying layers reporting up to the C-suite.

This may seem elementary to you, but early in my career—even when starting out at a Fortune 100 company—I was in the dark. Thankfully, I realized how understanding such structures was crucial to designing a long-term plan that would be exhilarating, realistic, and, most importantly, largely within my control.

This isn't to say there's some universal business structure all firms adhere to. How the financial technology sector organizes may be vastly different from pharma or hospitality, but there are enough consistencies to leverage as you set your sights beyond just what's next. Your career plan shouldn't focus solely on your next role but also the two, three, and four roles beyond that. If you truly want an intentional career, it means taking a long-term view of your professional arc, understanding the organizational infrastructure that will facilitate that arc, allowing for serendipity (as much or little as you'd like or can tolerate), and then putting your plan into action.

Backcasting and Forecasting to Design Your Career Map

I believe this mapping process is the single most important differentiator between careers that are accidental, meandering from company to company and job to job, and those that are intentional and following a well-charted course. Again, this isn't just a plan for the next role ahead but every role you want and need to accomplish along the path that leads to your ultimate career role, whatever that may be.

For me, that day in TGI Fridays, it was positioning myself to run for Congress in my late forties.

Before my stint at Disney, I'd spent several years working on political campaigns at the state, local, and national levels. I'd loved most of it and felt that someday I'd like to move beyond being a political strategist and operative to becoming a candidate myself. And I very much wanted to be a different type of candidate—one not beholden to special interests, PAC money, or desperate, nonstop fundraising. And *that* would require me to self-fund a campaign.

I set my sights on a 2016 race—yes, I planned a campaign some twenty-five years out. I figured by then, if I worked my multidecade career plan, I'd have built the net worth required to finance my run for office. I figured two million dollars should do it. I'd just save that over a few decades. (Hey, if I'm anything, I'm ambitious.)

I started on the right side of my plan and wrote "age 50" at the top of the far-right tick mark. Then I scribbled "congressman" in the space I reserved for title/role. I also added my salary, which I now know wouldn't cover the cost of a home and car in both my district and Washington, DC, which is why most members of Congress live college-style while in DC, with four to six of them sharing a house or apartment. I then added some blank lines at the bottom and titled them "What needs to occur before I land this role to actually make it happen?" That started the magic of what I've now mentored thousands of people to do: think of their career in terms of decades, begin with the ultimate end in mind, and then work backwards by *backcasting*.

Now, it's important to differentiate backcasting from forecasting. *Forecasting* is what most people will do when visioning. They decide what's next . . . typically immediately next. It takes vision to see what's beyond that. I hear so many people say, "I'm not creative" or "I'm not very visionary." I think that's a limiting mindset and flat-out wrong. We must nurture our creativity to become creative. We must practice having vision to become visionary. These are skills that can be developed. In fact, I believe everyone can develop these life and professional competencies. It may take an extraordinary level of discipline to employ a vision of what's beyond "next" for you, but you can do it.

I'd argue career planning is most decidedly more than a visioning exercise. It's also strategizing—only backwards. That's what I did. I decided that if I wanted to build the skills, knowledge, and wealth to campaign for a congressional seat, then the step before running for Congress was to be a CEO, or at least be in the C-suite for eight to ten years.

I then repeated the exercise with each role, continuing to move backwards: EVP, SVP, VP, general manager, senior director, director, manager . . . I wrote the title/role and the age at which I wanted to achieve it, combined with the date, the salary it should pay, and, most vitally, the skills I needed to build prior to that role in order to earn it on the timeline I'd absurdly and perhaps even arrogantly illustrated. My TGI

Fridays server, in his red-and-white striped shirt saddled with an abundance of buttons and pins, was so impressed with my multiyear plan, I remember what he said after I finished explaining it to him. "Wow—that's legit!"

I'll admit most of my planning seemed fun and even outrageous at the time. But it's been the blueprint for my career for three decades and counting. I've opened it multiple times a year, making slight adjustments, checking off milestones, and finding moments to celebrate. As my career took off, no one knew I had a hand-drawn map on the back of a grease-stained paper placemat detailing my deliberate career trajectory.

Except for me. Some guys my age carried around a "black book." I carried around my TGI Fridays long-term career plan. Nerd alert!

Of course, stuff happens along the way. Sometimes that stuff is simply serendipity. For me, I knew earning a seat in the C-suite meant I'd need lots of varied experiences, including at least one international assignment, direct revenue responsibility, marketing, and product development experience. I'd need to become proficient in reading a P&L and managing costs and margin, and I'd need to develop leadership skills, interviewing skills, and exiting and termination skills. I also had to learn how to create a culture in which people choose a high level of engagement and stay with the organization. Plus many other skills we read about on job descriptions and in leadership books and blogs. But reading about them and developing them are vastly different.

Not every assignment I applied for worked out, and I ended up moving to cities I didn't want to, but I came to appreciate the value of them all. It's important to note that on several occasions I sought and earned assignments that were way outside my comfort zone, sometimes not especially appealing, and mostly a massive stretch for my skill set at the time. But every one of them was ultimately aligned with progressing me down my planned career path.

I want to reiterate that this skill isn't unique to me. I'm not any smarter or better educated or more talented than you. In fact, you're probably more educated and more talented than I am, given the nature of the world some of you who are younger than me may have grown up in. My point is, move outside your comfort zone and see the resulting stretch required as a necessary opportunity, not a limiting obstacle to your intentional career journey.

Leave Room for the Unexpected and Recalibrate as Needed

No matter how grandiose your career plan, you must leave space for the realities of life. Relationships begin and end. Recessions come and go. Change arrives, both planned and unplanned. Leave some breathing room in your plan as you consider what might happen, what's likely to happen, and what fairly predictably happens. That way, when new industries emerge or life circumstances shift, your plan can be substantially altered at a moment's notice. Plan for your plan to be disrupted, and then you won't be shocked or hamstrung when it is. Instead, you'll be prepared to pivot to another opportunity along your forecasted timeline. The fact is, all careers have a reality of two steps forward, one step back. Or some lateral movement or emotional disruption will be forced upon you that you'll need to react to. Expect it, anticipate it, prepare for it, and act on it.

You may be wondering what happened to my congressional career. Well, their names are Stephanie, Thatcher, Smith, and

Wentworth. Spending half of my time in Washington, DC, and 100 percent of my time in the public eye was not congruent with making my future family a priority, so as much as it was a significant career goal of mine, I had to pivot to serve a greater constituency. (And by greater, I mean one that wouldn't stalk, harass, or, in some cases, try to murder me. It may sound crazy, but in reality, it's all too true. Public service has come to repel many people like myself, and that's sad.)

The accompanying exercise, similar to your Team of Eight work in the previous chapter, likely requires more than a trip to the coffee shop to fill it all in. And, yes, I know I drew mine on the back of a placemat in one sitting, but I've also spent several decades thinking about it and consistently tweaking it, so I'm providing you with a more thoughtful framework to fill out than I had. It will take time and will benefit from multiple iterations as you determine how one role proceeds to the next and the skills required to do so. I strongly recommend you meet with people who hold each of these identified roles and ask them what skills they mastered prior to being promoted. Be certain not to glean a list of thirty things from their entire career but rather to focus on what they needed to learn and master most consequentially when moving from director to senior director, or from SVP to EVP, or whatever the titles might be for your specific employer and industry.

You will see on the worksheet that there's space for up to six skills needed for each role. These are skills you should master to ensure you're qualified to move from one role to the next. So, although you're initially building your plan by backcasting, moving from right to left and stopping where you are now, you'll reverse direction as you identify the skills needed for each role, moving left to right. Thus, the best practice for your career plan is to backcast and then forecast—don't worry, the worksheet will make it easy.

Keep in mind that this long-term plan is for your eyes only unless you choose to share it. Like the foundational exercise in Strategy 1 around your personal and professional values, resist the temptation to select future roles and milestones based on how you think they might look to someone else. It's understandable why that might creep into your planning, but you're not here to impress anyone else. This is *your* plan, and you alone are the one to create it and find value in it. Which isn't to say you can't benefit from reviewing it with a mentor or even someone in your network or organization whose journey followed a similar path. That's where more recalibration might come into play.

I recognize you don't know where you'll be working nine months from now, let alone nine years. Just do your best. Calibrate your plan with seasoned colleagues who can help you identify logical role progressions, reasonable time frames, income expectations, and specific skills you need to gain to ensure your continued progression.

············ **EXERCISE SETUP** ············

Illustrate and Recalibrate Your Long-Term Plan

I consider this exercise to be the centerpiece of both this book and the Career on Course online resource. It provides a framework to think strategically about your long-term plan and determine the roles, skills, talents, and promotions you need to deliberately create your career path.

Remember, this plan requires both backcasting and forecasting. Forecasting is often focused on what's immediately ahead of you. This strategy is indisputably valuable, but it needs to be complemented by backcasting: looking longer term—decades longer—and setting your eye on the "ultimate prize." Once you've identified that, you can plan backward to illustrate specific career milestones you need to secure this future. If your ultimate career goal isn't readily in sight, start with your present role and forecast it forward as far as you can.

Take your time on your long-term plan. You will likely revisit and recalibrate it many times along your career journey. To complete your own plan, follow these steps and refer to the example on pp. 114–15.

- Fill in the date boxes using three-to-five-year increments. Each box represents a core milestone in your career journey. If you choose to backcast, complete the far-right date box first to represent your final career milestone. But feel free to start with any date box on the long-term plan.
- Record the age you will be at each career milestone. For example, if you're currently thirty-two, your final milestone might be thirty years from now, and your age at the top will be sixty-two.
- Record the job title or role you intend to have at each milestone. Also note the compensation you plan to earn in each job title or role.
- Most importantly, list both the technical and social/interpersonal skills you will need to master in each role. Mastering one role earns you the right to move to the next. Consider interviewing a credible person who currently holds each role about the skill sets you'll need to be successful at each point on your long-term plan.

Illustrate and Recalibrate Your Long-Term Plan

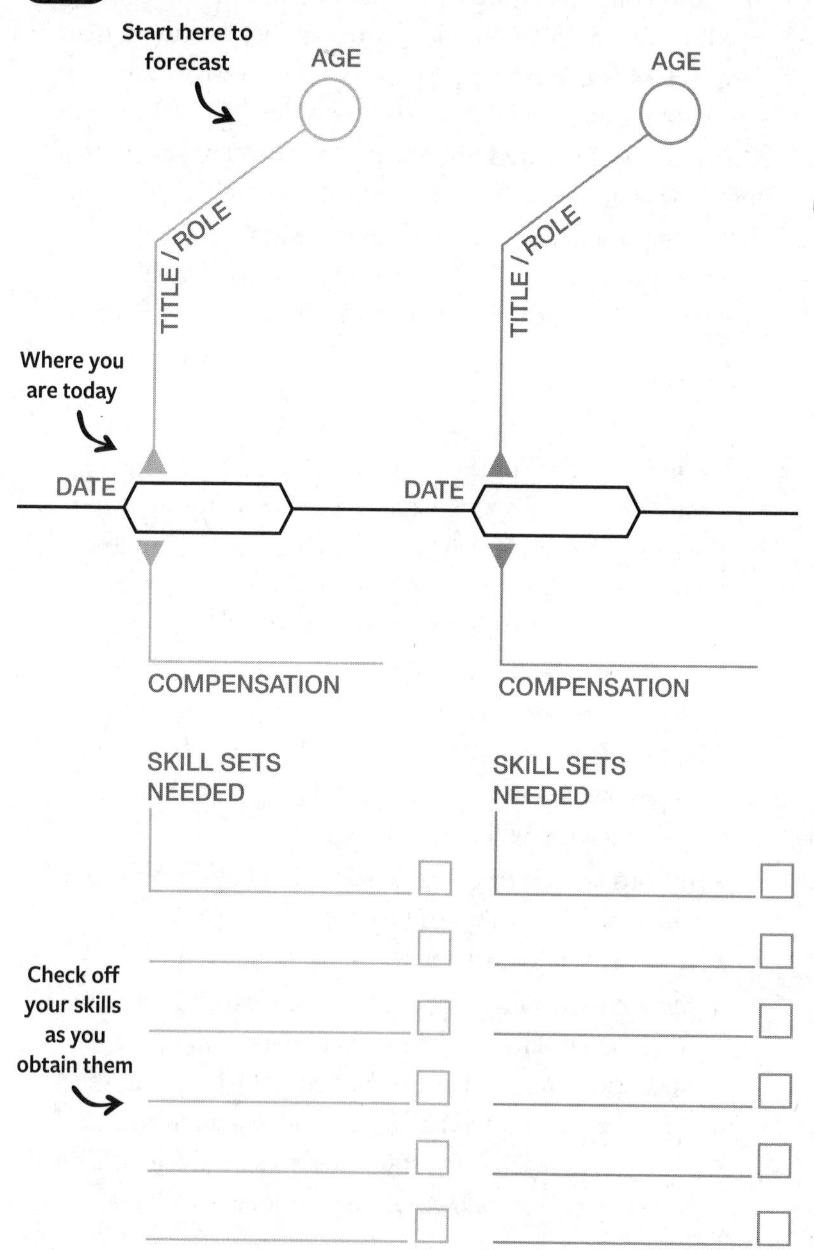

As you forecast your future career milestones, research the skill sets or experience required for the next levels up in your long-term plan.

AGE

TITLE / ROLE

DATE

COMPENSATION

SKILL SETS NEEDED

AGE

TITLE / ROLE

DATE

COMPENSATION

SKILL SETS NEEDED

These skill sets may be years or decades away from building, but it's useful to have them in your line of sight.

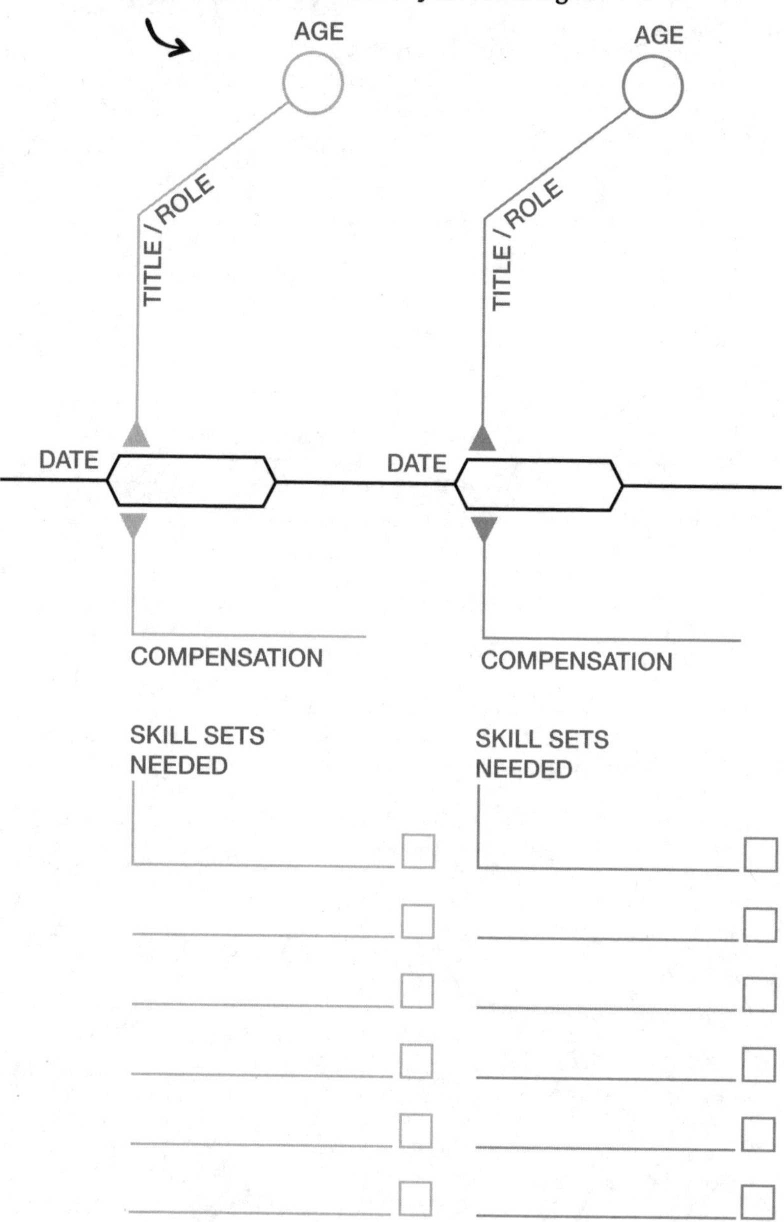

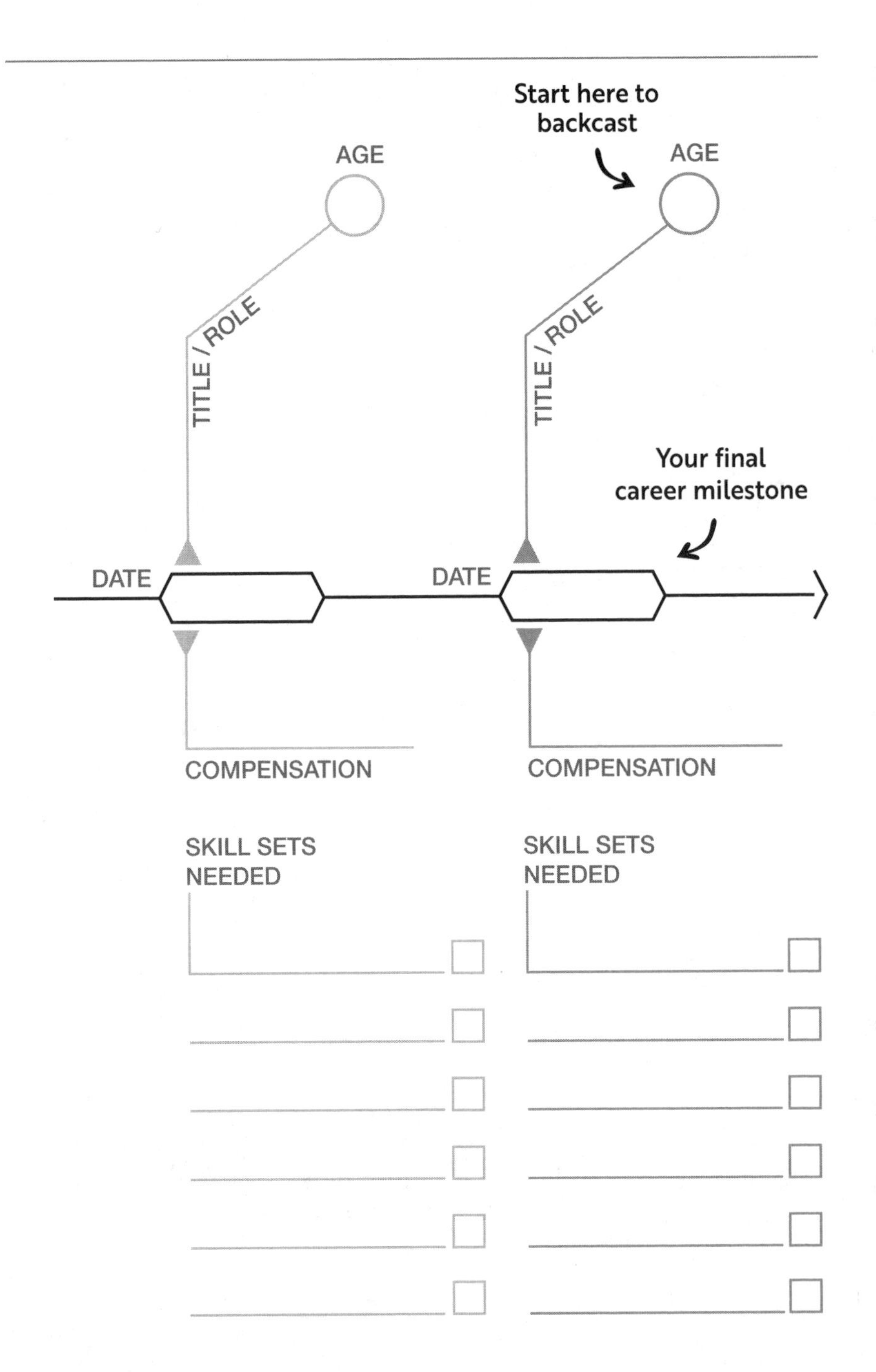

Start here to backcast
AGE
TITLE / ROLE
DATE
COMPENSATION
SKILL SETS NEEDED
AGE
TITLE / ROLE
Your final career milestone
DATE
COMPENSATION
SKILL SETS NEEDED

STRATEGY 4 Illustrate and Recalibrate Your Long-Term Plan

Example Page

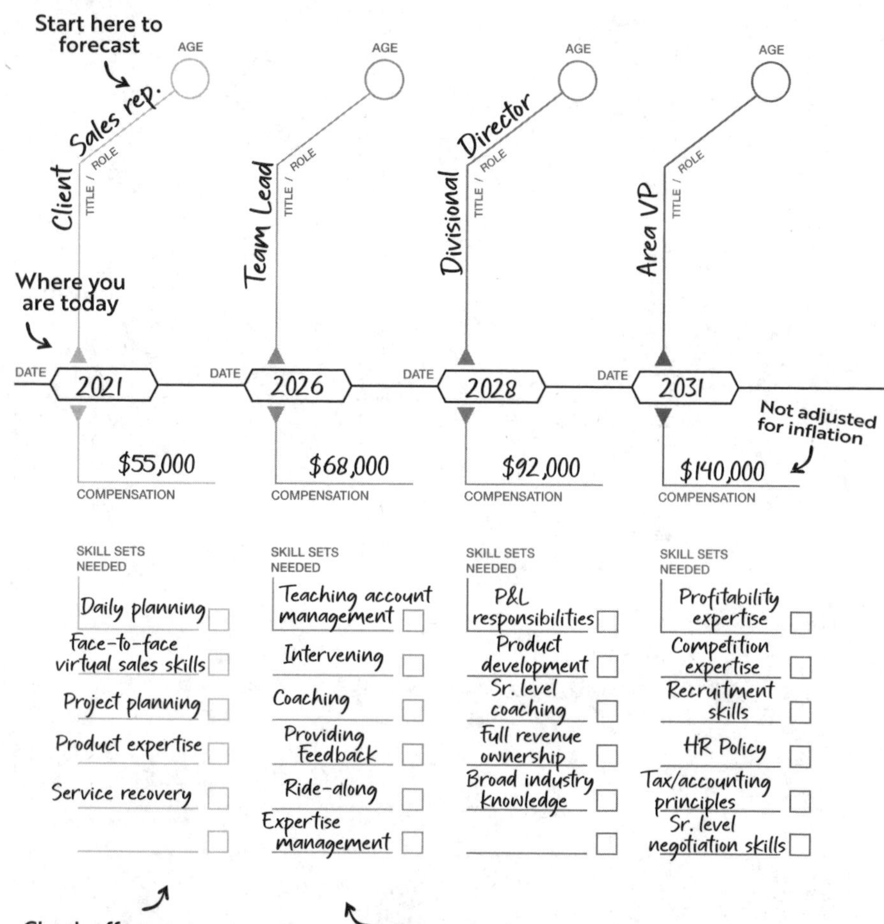

Check off your skills as you obtain them

As you forecast your future career milestones, research the skill sets or experience required for the next levels up in your long-term plan.

Example Page

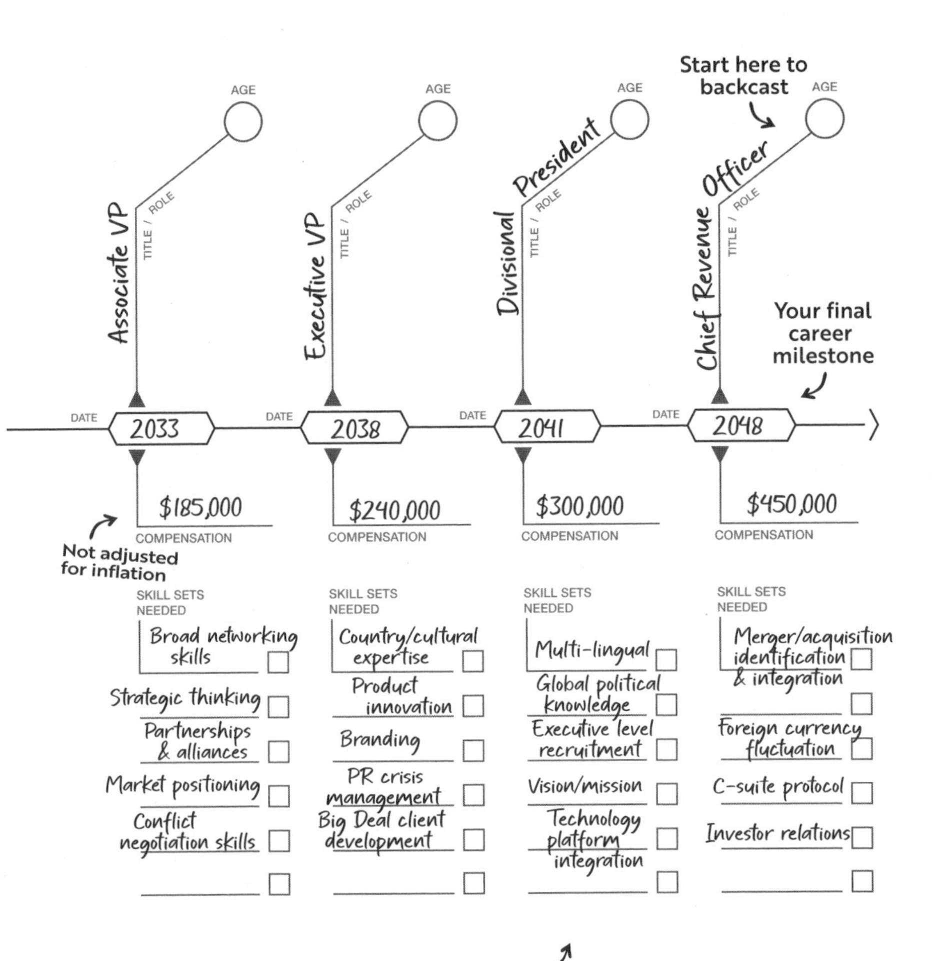

These skill sets may be years or decades away from building, but it's useful to have them in your line of sight.

STRATEGY

5

Define and Build Your Brand

Defining and building a personal brand is a vital step in furthering your career. Your brand can help you stand out in a competitive job market, increase your visibility to potential employers, and create a lasting impression that can serve you well. As such, your brand will reflect your values, achievements, and skills. A well-crafted brand will help differentiate you from others and show potential leaders that you're the right fit for the next role in your career progression. Further, building a positive brand helps you foster and sustain meaningful relationships with colleagues, mentors, and other professionals, increasing your credibility and expanding your professional network. This may all seem like platitudes, but it's indisputably true.

However you ultimately craft your brand, it's vital to be intentional with the message you want to convey about yourself. Start by considering the qualities and experiences that make you unique, then ponder how these traits would be perceived by others. Drawing on your work in Strategy 1, use your values lists as the foundation of your branding efforts to build a public case for who you are and what you stand for. But there's an often-overlooked responsibility that comes with defining and building your brand that goes directly to leadership.

Make It Safe for Others to Tell You the (Hard) Truth

After more than three decades dedicated to leadership, organizational culture, mentoring, and career development, I've staked out a position on what I think a leader's two most vital contributions are. Okay, maybe they're the second and third most vital, as we know leaders must set vision and strategy first—especially at the top. But before developing systems, structures, processes, and the like, leaders must develop, master, and elevate the competencies of (1) Identifying talent and (2) Providing feedback.

Identifying talent via proper recruitment and retainment is likely the largest and most impactful contribution a leader can make. You can be a creative genius, have all the funding in the world, and possess the most innovative and brilliant go-to-market strategy, but if you don't have the right people on board to execute it and refine it, nothing matters.

Leaders who focus on recruiting alone often fall a bit short, as they forget that once they've hired the best talent, the clock starts ticking on how long that person will choose to stay engaged and ignore or delay the onslaught of recruiters trying to poach them. Building a culture where people feel valued, heard, seen, felt, wanted, and rewarded is a foundational principle of every leader's career. It's an environment where people stay and resist the constant temptation of "the grass is always greener on the other side."

Second to identifying talent through recruitment and retention is providing feedback. It's not only a leadership imperative but one of the greatest gifts a leader can give to their team members—especially feedback on their blind spots. This is precisely the reason you must engage proactively with *your* leader to chart your career. Not only must you be mindful of the brand you're building for yourself—and you are building a brand, even if you're not aware of what it is—you also should seek honest validating and corrective feedback from others about it.

It's your job to make it safe for your leader to give you feedback in service of your career objectives. We reviewed this concept in Strategy 3: Study Yourself, but I'm revisiting it to elevate its importance. Remember, for most people, being on the "giving" end of feedback is one of the most intimidating and potentially unsafe things they can be asked to do. But since this is *your* career, and you're asking for feedback in service of *your* goals, be sure to make it easy and comfortable for your leader to do so. You will likely need to step up and invite feedback from others for it to happen—including your leader. The fact that someone is a leader doesn't correlate to their having the courage and diplomacy to provide others with unsolicited productive feedback. Too many leaders I encounter say they don't do so for fear of hurting the feelings of their team member. To that I say: it's incumbent on every leader to summon the courage to take on the undiscussables and provide your team members with feedback on their behavior and brand.

While it can be rough seeking feedback, it's the receiving part where things can really get difficult. But being on the receiving end of such feedback is how we all grow and mature. One of the biggest complaints I hear from people when a friendship ends, they're passed over for a promotion, they hear a criticism of their skills, or they learn from a third party about a personality trait that offended or annoyed someone is "Well, I wished they'd told me. Why didn't they just tell me this to my face?"

Such a sentiment is very naive. Whatever our overall brand is or becomes, it must include being the kind of person who makes it safe and comfortable for others to tell us their truth. The hard truth. That's something most of us don't do well and, as a result, we lack the understanding of what it's really like to be in a relationship with us.

Vital reminder here: this is *your* responsibility, not someone else's. If people aren't telling you the truth—their truth—about how they feel about you, that says more about you than it does about them. Sorry for the sobering slap, but this advice will serve you immensely well in life, both personally and professionally. This is how you understand what your brand is and how you make it what you want it to be—and there's *always* a disconnect. Always. With rare exceptions, you've behaved yourself into the reputation and brand that you have, and only *you* can behave yourself out of it.

Building Self-Awareness Is Foundational to Building Your Brand

The only way to maximize the value of this chapter is to complete, or at least make some legitimate progress, with your Team of Eight exercise from Strategy 3. The outcome is a realistic composite of not only how you see yourself but how others see you—and by now you've learned there's often a vast chasm between the two. If not, you're probably kidding yourself and should pick other team members who will talk straight to you about what it's like to be in your orbit.

From the ongoing process of building your self-awareness, you're also building a sense for your brand—or most importantly, how others see your brand. That you have a brand should not be a new concept. You have either intentionally created your brand with care and deliberation or, like most of us, left it to chance as an accumulation of both positive and self-defeating behaviors. Rarely has someone created a positive brand accidentally. It may feel like you have, but if so you're likely fooling yourself. Without intentionality, you're mindlessly creating and shaping your brand with every conversation, response, reaction, question, statement, email, phone call, Zoom meeting, team retreat, group collaboration, social post, and feedback session. Every interaction you have either reinforces or changes your brand for better or worse.

I recently watched an interview on NBC featuring Adam Grant, bestselling author of *Think Again*, and he reinforced an idea he also shared as a tweet: "Listen to the advice you give to others. It's usually the advice you need to take yourself."[1] I mention this because the principle is profound: it's easier for us to assess other people's brands than our own. However, a competency common to intentional careers is understanding our own brand and determining, as objectively as possible, how aligned it is with what our employer values.

Think about the people you work with daily. I bet, like me, it's easy for you to assess their brand in a sentence or two based on your consistent interactions with them. For example:

- The technically competent individual who never commits to a deadline and later feigns ignorance that you've ever stated one. Also adept at playing devil's advocate and is a contrarian at every point. It's fatiguing. It's also their brand.

- The colleague with a remarkable ability to leave a meeting with an assignment, head to their office, close the door for four hours, and emerge with the entire thing completed. Zero interruptions, phone calls, emails, or social media posts—nothing distracts them from completing the project as promised. They're dependable, efficient, and highly effective. And likewise, it's also their brand.
- The team member who is flexible and willing to help others, pitching in to cover for absent colleagues and willing to do anything asked of them, including changing roles for extended periods of high pressure. However, text or call them after hours or on weekends and they shut you down with strict boundaries on when, if at all, they will talk after "normal" business hours. Sometimes appreciated and sometimes resented, it's also their brand.
- The associate who out of the gate rejects, dismisses, and disparages any creative campaign that they're not involved in from the beginning. If they weren't part of the original scoping, then it's dead on arrival. You can count on it every time. Predictably laughable, and it's also their brand.
- The leader who first carefully listens to everyone's opinion and then, after everyone feels heard, shares their own—never first but always last. Empowering and trusting, which also becomes their brand.

- The executive leader who, in a misguided attempt to be inclusive, encourages all meeting attendees to share and debate all opinions, even though they've made their decision before the meeting even begins. They never intend to change their mind and simply need to summon the courage to exercise executive privilege and announce "I've made a decision that I need everyone to support. I don't want anyone's opinion on the decision, but I do want your knowledge and expertise on how to best execute it." Instead, they're indecisive and disingenuous, wasting time on what could be better deployed on topics that are, in fact, open for discussion. This is their brand.

The above should validate how easy it is to call associates to mind and clearly articulate their brands. Understandably, recognizing our own brands proves more difficult. Personally, it's how I've been able to list the highly rewarding and simultaneously embarrassing traits that comprise my overall brand. Further in this chapter, I've candidly listed a fairly exhaustive and sometimes shocking collection of my own behaviors based on how I see my own brand and also drawn from the collective feedback of my previous leaders.

I'll go ahead and turn the lens on myself, as I think I'm sufficiently self-aware at this point in my life, though I recognize my wife might disagree. But her frustration aside, here's how I think my brand is perceived:

- I'm impulsive. My bias toward action is both a strength to motivate myself and others to execute on strategy, but sometimes I can be viewed as the type of leader who shouts: "Ready . . . Fire! . . . Aim . . ."

- I need a better filter between what I say and what I think. As an outward processor, I need better verbal restraint. Always.
- I enjoy a deep reservoir of creativity. It's rarely a bad thing, unless I'm being the "smartest person in the room" and overshadowing the genius of others. Which I do frequently.
- I'm a great communicator, an adept negotiator, and remarkably persuasive. Sometimes irresponsibly so.
- I think I'm nearly always right. If you'd just listen more carefully to my wisdom (passion), you'd see the genius in my argument.
- I am fiercely loyal. Even if you're not to me.
- I have great taste. This includes hotels, vacations, food, champagne, clothes, cars, and so on. And as long as I'm paying, how can there be a downside? Except for when it becomes a bit "showy"—which my oldest son now accuses me of weekly. Yes, I'm being parented by my thirteen-year-old.
- I find it very hard to focus on narrowing my priorities, options, and projects.
- I think bigger is better. Always. And it isn't.
- I generally like to see others succeed, and it shows in my leadership style, social posts, and the talent agency I co-own.
- I'm contagiously positive. Which is fatiguing for some.
- I can't be trusted to keep a secret. If you want it to remain a secret, don't tell me. But if you want it strategically leaked, I'm your guy!

- My actions align with a spirit and a reputation of gratitude.
- I can be petty. I'm sometimes jealous. I can absolutely be vindictive. I've been told I'm quite shallow.
- I'm that friend you call at three in the morning to bail you out. In times of crisis, natural disasters, or family trauma, I'll be the first one there to help.
- If you give me a task, consider it done. I can always be counted on to do more than my share.
- I don't have to always be the lead. I'm quite good at taking direction and following competent, visionary people.
- I don't burn bridges. I can count on one hand the number of broken friendships I've had in fifty-five years.
- I'm remarkably forgiving. And I expect you to offer me the same courtesy.
- I'm very comfortable with interpersonal conflict. So much so that I'm known for searching it out.
- I'm quite fearless professionally. Self-disruption is my strength.

Oh, I could've typed for hours, people. I've done some work on the self-awareness side and have a pretty clear idea of what my brand is with other people, positively and negatively. Notice I didn't say *neutrally*. You're either all-in or all-out with Scott Jeffrey Miller.

If anything, I hope reading the above makes you feel safe to be completely transparent and honest about your brand. If I can lay myself bare in a book that my friends, neighbors, coworkers, family, champions, and haters will all read, then I invite you to embrace the same level of vulnerability. Do some work on your self-awareness. This is both a simple and often painful exercise, correlated with your level of maturity. You'll notice that at least 50 percent of the brand attributes I identified weren't very flattering. In fact, even when I paid myself a compliment, I shared the likely downside. Because we know all strengths and assets, when overplayed, can become weaknesses and liabilities.

When I think about the brand I want to have, as viewed by others, this is what my list would ideally look like:

- Unfailingly keeps promises.
- Overdelivers results on time and on budget.
- Prioritizes well and balances strategy with tactics.
- Exhibits high energy without overshadowing others.
- Demonstrates a noticeable balance of speaking and listening.
- Is well informed and judicious with opinions.
- Can be trusted like a lockbox to keep confidences. (Who am I kidding? This isn't ever going to be my brand.)

Not All Brands Are Complex—But They Should All Be Strategic

Some brands are quite simple—and not in a bad way at all. I know people who, when I think of their brand, my first thought would be *punctual*, *minimalist*, *forgiving*, *reasonable*, *wise*, *organized*, *quiet*, *stylish*, or even *consistent sender of thank-you notes*. Not all brands need to be elaborate and complex, but they should be strategically thought out and planned. And it's never too late to build the brand you want.

I've dedicated the exercise in this chapter to four distinct activities and learnings:

- How you see your brand.
- How others see your brand.
- What type of brand you want for yourself.
- What you can do about it.

For many of the exercises throughout this book, you'll need to solicit feedback and opinions from others. Who you ask is ultimately your decision, but be mindful that if you keep going back to the same handful of people, they're going to get fatigued. Carefully contemplate who you will ask for the second part of this exercise—you want the insights to be varied, relevant, and current.

I suspect the value of this strategy is implicit in its title, Define and Build Your Brand. In my professional experience, those with the most intentional and successful careers are fastidious about their brands. They're calculated and not cavalier. They consider the impact and consequences of what they say and how they behave. In short, they're self-aware and know what it's like to work with them. Here's the big idea: the most intentional careers result from the most self-aware people.

As you're building your self-awareness around your brand, keep in mind the brand you're striving for. One of irreverence and impetuousness? This might be exactly what's needed if you're a comedian, podcaster, radio host, or actor. But in a more buttoned-up corporate culture, your peers and boss may see you as uninvested or as using humor to mask outright hostility. Every organization and culture values and rejects specific brands, so you need to determine if the brand you have and the brand you want fit your current circumstances.

And don't guess if it's a fit. Ask a trusted leader in human resources or people services what's valued in the organization. A great question is literally, "As you think about those people who've had the most successful careers here, what commonalities do you see in their personal brands?" Then shut up, listen, and write what they say word for word. Then and only then can you decide if you want to emulate those people's brands or not.

EXERCISE SETUP

Define and Build Your Brand

You already have a brand. But as we discussed in this chapter, what you think it is may not be the same as what others think it is. Nor is there any guarantee that your current brand is the one that will best serve your career. Acknowledge that we all have some level of disconnect between how we view ourselves and how others view us as you complete the following exercises.

Be Introspective

On page 130 are ten spaces for writing single words that describe how you see your current brand. These words should include positive (complimentary) and negative (critical) descriptions. If they're all positive or mostly vague, revisit Strategy 3: Study Yourself. Make these words bold, specific, insightful, deliberate, and actionable descriptions of how you see your brand. The bolder and more specific they are, the better.

Learn from Three Others

Next, ask three people to share up to ten single words to describe how they see your personal brand. They may or may not be part of your Team of Eight. It's your call. Make sure you help them understand what you mean by *brand*. You may also want them to expand on the words they list for further context; that's your choice. But ultimately, they should offer simple and brief responses. Don't pressure them to stretch it to ten. Less can be more, and offering feedback can be overwhelming for anyone who hasn't been in a position to practice this type of interplay. Be certain your three people also offer some negative or critical branding terms, or their lavish praise of you will be useless.

Identify Your Desired Brand

Once you've gathered enough perspective, identify your desired brand in the respective column on page 132. These final words should be profound to you, key actionable words to build the brand you want. Although there are lines on the worksheet to accommodate up to ten potential words, I recommend you limit yourself to three to five words. Any more than that and it will be impossible to integrate them all into your future behaviors.

Define Actions

In the final column on page 132, identify the behaviors that, when taken, will demonstrate you're living your desired brand. Specifically list what you will do more of, do less of, or do entirely differently to accomplish your brand—in your eyes and the eyes of others.

Define and Build Your Brand

How do I see my brand?	*How do others see my brand?*		
MYSELF	*PERSON 1*	*PERSON 2*	*PERSON 3*
O ______	O ______	O ______	O ______
O ______	O ______	O ______	O ______
O ______	O ______	O ______	O ______
O ______	O ______	O ______	O ______
O ______	O ______	O ______	O ______
O ______	O ______	O ______	O ______
O ______	O ______	O ______	O ______
O ______	O ______	O ______	O ______
O ______	O ______	O ______	O ______
O ______	O ______	O ______	O ______

Use these sample traits to describe your future brand on the next page.

- Accommodating
- Accountable
- Accurate
- Adaptable
- Ambitious
- Brave
- Calm
- Collaborative
- Consistent
- Creative
- Credible
- Dedicated
- Deliberate
- Dependable
- Dynamic
- Efficient

What do I want my brand to be?	***What can I do, or stop doing, to fulfill my brand?***
○ ______________________	○ ______________________
○ ______________________	○ ______________________
○ ______________________	○ ______________________
○ ______________________	○ ______________________
○ ______________________	○ ______________________
○ ______________________	○ ______________________
○ ______________________	○ ______________________
○ ______________________	○ ______________________
○ ______________________	○ ______________________
○ ______________________	○ ______________________

Empathic
Exacting
Fearless
Ferocious
Generous
Grateful
Harmonious
Helpful
Honorable
Industrious
Innovative
Just
Kind/Caring
Knowledgeable
Loyal
Mature
Methodical
Nice
Nimble
Patient
Problem-Solving
Progressive
Punctual
Reflective
Relentless
Resourceful
Self-Assured
Strategic
Stylish
Trusted
Vivacious
Well-Spoken

STRATEGY

Be Willing to Disrupt Yourself

All the strategies in this book require self-reflection and an investment of time into each of the concepts to bring them to life in your career. Several also require a level of courage that might not come naturally for you. Get ready, because being willing to disrupt yourself will demand such courage.

I opened Strategy 4 by sharing the best career advice I have: illustrate and recalibrate your long-term plan. With the emergence of microcareers becoming increasingly shorter inside specific organizations, it's realistic and even likely that by the time you finish the professional phase of your life, some of you will have had upward of twenty different organizational experiences. Think about it: For an average career, you'll be working full-time for about forty to forty-five years. And if the new norm of an eighteen-month average per job continues, that means many of you may have *thirty different jobs* over the course of your career! With thirty different organizations, in thirty different cultures, working for thirty different leaders.

The Rise of Microcareers

The ever-changing nature of the digital economy has further revolutionized how work is done. No longer confined to traditional corporate structures, many find themselves navigating microcareers—short-term projects and engagements that allow them to build a wide portfolio of experience and knowledge. This new landscape presents both opportunities and challenges for career momentum. As organizations have become increasingly agile and open to experimenting with new methods and approaches to work, those charting intentional careers can benefit by adopting a similar level of agility. The ability to adapt quickly while cultivating a new set of skills can help expand your capabilities, expose you to new ways of problem-solving, and introduce you to new and valuable contacts from diverse industries. Engaging in a higher number of microcareers can also provide the freedom to chart a path that connects with projects or work you find personally interesting and motivating. But of course, this changing landscape comes with its share of downsides.

One of the primary drawbacks with microcareers is that they often lack the job security and stability that come with more traditional careers. This means you can find yourself in a precarious position if your project or engagement fails to pan out as expected or ends prematurely. And you may have to be satisfied with less or sporadic pay due to the shorter terms and lack of commitment on behalf of employers, not to mention not qualifying for benefits such as health insurance or retirement plans typically offered through more traditional employment.

So while this growing era of microcareers can offer increased flexibility and career opportunities, it also requires a great deal of dedication to ensure success. Depending on your point of view, you may find that exhilarating or crushing. And to the degree this becomes your career reality, you'll need to develop a level of mental, emotional, and skill agility previously unheard of. Not impossible, just not the norm for previous generations. It's a huge wake-up call to think you may have twenty to thirty disruptive microcareers in front of you.

Be the Disrupter by Choosing Value-Based Behaviors

But the real question is, Who is doing the disruption? If you can't guess by the title of this strategy, the disrupter should be *you*. But before I prepare you to build and refine the muscles of self-disruption, I'd like to remind you just how much your career will be disrupted by forces outside your control. As I mentioned in the introduction, this quote from my colleague should both haunt and motivate you: "You are never in the room when your career is decided for you." So offensive and so true.

I've referenced several times—okay, pretty much nonstop throughout this book—that the bulk of my own career was inside the FranklinCovey Company. I spent much of the first half of my tenure working with Dr. Covey himself, traveling with him to client events, interviewing him on videos, and laughing with him about life as a Catholic in Provo, Utah. They were truly magical times of learning from the master of all mentors. Of the many profound things I learned from him, it was the power of developing a proactive mindset that may have been the most impactful for me. In fact, it's the basis for Habit 1 in his book *The 7 Habits of Highly Effective People*. I think most people think being proactive means taking charge and being in control. Leading out. Showing initiative. And they're right. Do all of that. Talk about great career and life advice.

But Dr. Covey focused on a different view: that proactive, highly effective people are simply not reactive. They build the maturity, discipline, and focus *not* to react to others—their moods, desires, needs, or agendas. Metaphorically, they "carry their own weather." They don't choose their responses to others based on anyone else's moods, feelings, or other external circumstances but rather on their own values. They wear this insight and maturity as a shield in day-to-day situations where an onslaught of challenges, bad news, and difficult people with ridiculous levels of anger and immaturity often come zinging in like bullets.

His counsel seems like a great way to live your life, doesn't it? But it's insanely hard and humbling. As an author and speaker, I've spent seemingly endless hours on planes, traveling millions of miles over a lifetime. Planes are hot boxes of emotion. They're high-flying pressure cookers that vex us with reclined seats resting on our knees, missed connections, interrupted movies, multihour tarmac delays, unavailable Wi-Fi, overhead bin space wars, and, perhaps the most incendiary of all, snack shortages. That's not even bothering with the passenger with the peanut allergy, the bad weather bouncing the aircraft around, or the passenger who's had too much alcohol. You name the pressure and it's like Moore's Law on an airplane: every slight, or perceived slight, is massively magnified.

The most boorish behavior I've ever seen in my entire life is from passengers in first class. Usually having to do with their meal. It is truly gross. No, not the meal. Their ingratitude.

The reason I share this is I've been in numerous situations where tensions were near explosive. After a three-hour grounding on the tarmac, I'm talking about men standing up and threatening to rush the cockpit or open the door and jump out. Seriously. People screaming and punching each other over some argument and agreeing to meet at the baggage claim to settle it later. Again, I'm not making this up. And yet, despite my many trips in this emotional and high-flying pressure cooker, I still never give up the ability to choose my response to every situation I'm put in. Do I choose to escalate or de-escalate? Bring levity or crush the other person with a lightning-fast verbal assault? Assume good intent and show some unwarranted mercy or, well, not? We never lose our ability to choose our response in a situation, despite the number of emotional arrows flung our way.

The lesson here is to build your proactive muscle but never forget life is 10 percent what happens to you and 90 percent how you react to it, as the saying goes. Take a moment and let that sink in. You can't believe how empowering and liberating that mantra can become, mainly to your emotional and mental health. Because you will lose your job, miss out on a promotion, be discriminated against, and feel screwed over more than once. And the more you know all of these situations are inevitable, the less they'll catch you off guard and hijack your focus and long-term plan.

Which is to say, the first discipline of self-disruption is guarding yourself against *other* disruptions. If you can't marshal the discipline to control how you react to the world around you, you won't be able to reach deep at those critical inflection points in your career and have the presence and fortitude to disrupt yourself.

Embrace the fact that other people disrupting you is absolutely coming your way, and the more you expect it, the less you need to be unsettled by it. It never ceases to amaze me the shock some people experience when their job is eliminated, and I saw it coming for months. I'm not clairvoyant—I just have my head out of the sand and, because I'm expecting change, I can quickly catch the telltale signs. The more you anticipate and embrace that change and disruption are happening all the time and that your turn is coming, the less it will shock you and the more you'll be prepared for it.

I board every plane knowing there could be a fight or some near altercation. That the Wi-Fi will likely not work or my movie will be reset twice. That my luggage will likely not fit into the overhead bin and, because my previous connection was late and I boarded last, I'll be forced to have my carry-on bag checked to my final destination. I'm just prepared for all of this, and then when it doesn't happen, I'm always delighted. It's a great way to live! Thank you, Dr. Covey. You've certainly saved me from ulcers and perhaps a punch in the jaw at the baggage claim.

When my job is eliminated, or someone acts upon me, or some massive disruption comes my way, I'm able to psychologically absorb it and pivot to my plan B or plan C immediately. Because quite frankly, I've been working on it all along. And so can you.

Know Your Expiration Date

Let's talk about self-disruption.

Next to my placemat story in TGI Fridays thirty-plus years ago, this concept is the most impactful of every strategy I've employed in my career to stay in control of my trajectory, maintain my momentum, and accelerate the progression of my long-term plan. Often called a career lifespan or job shelf life, it signifies that you're solely responsible for knowing your own expiration or "use by" date. Just like a freshly baked blueberry muffin left to sit for too long, you'll also get stale in a particular role.

Enter Whitney Johnson, who is a prolific author. Her book *Disrupt Yourself* is a must-read on your journey to becoming more deliberate with your career decisions.[1] A key takeaway from Johnson's research is about the lifespan of any job or role, which she proposes is about three years for most senior leaders, and increasingly more like eighteen months for most entry-level to mid-level associates. That exact time frame may not resonate precisely with you, but the fact is most of us don't consciously know when our expiration date is up. Others seem to, however, and often sense it even before we do. And when that "other" is your leader, they may see a bullseye on your back. Not always for termination or demotion but often for change that may not align with your own intentional multiyear career strategy.

Johnson also argues that after about three years into a job or role, we have mastered the key skills we initially found challenging and exhilarating. Once our learning curve is over, we can become subconsciously complacent. This isn't an accusation that we're "phoning it in" but rather acknowledging a natural tendency to become comfortable when we're not at the peak of our individual challenges. The issue is that others tend to notice it before we do, and that rarely bodes well for our brands and longevity. Now, certainly superb leaders recognize this reality and deliberately move high performers before any sense of role atrophy sets in, as they know that's when associates are most likely to be recruited and poached by the competition. But not all of us work with superb leaders, which is why we need to own our disruption.

We will all face disruption in our lives, some self-initiated but most externally created. Your job is to minimize the external disruptions as much as possible. Of course, you can't entirely insulate yourself and your career from all such disruptions, and perhaps you shouldn't. I often say the best days of my life were when I was hired into new organizations; the second-best days were the ones I was fired. Okay, maybe the day after, when the shock or panic had worn off and I realized how unhappy and trapped I'd been in the role but had lacked the courage to move myself out.

Act or be acted upon should become a professional mantra for us all. At some point, the odds of you being acted upon will decrease in direct correlation to your own willingness to act upon yourself—also known as self-disruption—first. When you act, others don't need to or aren't even able to. But when you don't self-disrupt, you can become a target for others to do so for you.

On you.

Against you.

This may seem simple on the surface, but I just described the reason for most terminations. The lesson here is to not surrender the decisions over your career to anyone else. It's just like in eighth grade when you learned your crush was going to break up with you at the playground after school, so you beat them to the punch and publicly broke up with them over lunch in the cafeteria for everyone to see. Okay, perhaps that's too much personal sharing, but you get the point—there's power in being the one in control.

In the twenty-five years I worked for FranklinCovey, I had nine distinct careers. They were completely different roles, often in different cities, states, and countries. Not everyone builds most of their career in one organization or even wants to. You may have upward of two dozen careers, and I don't stake any position on what your number should be. Mine is over fourteen, and I'm in my midfifties with twenty more years ahead of me. You might wonder, *Wait . . . Scott is working until he's seventy-four?* Yep, that's the plan. I have three young sons who apparently need braces, want to go to basketball and tennis camps, and have the audacity to show an interest in higher education.

I want your focus to be less on how many jobs, roles, and careers you'll have and more on achieving them at your direction and not someone else's. Whether that means a slew of microcareers, a carefully charted progression through a number of small organizations, or strategic upward progress in a Fortune 50—the choice is yours.

In Strategy 4, you invested the time to create the first draft of your multidecade timeline, so you should have a clearer sense now of the overall number and duration of each role you'll have. I recognize that it's a guess, but a "guessed at" plan is always, *always* better than no plan at all.

Depending on your generation and how well you relate to your peer age group, I think it's reasonable to generalize that the older you are, the more likely you are to fear disruption compared to younger generations such as Gen Z and Gen Y. Boomers, Gen Xers, and Millennials experienced a unique blend of family structures and values, world stability, accelerated innovation, and a cultural shift for how society sees risk and entrepreneurialism, fueling pressure for their children to follow a prescribed path.

I speak for many of my peers, as it was surprising and even shameful for us to hear someone graduating from high school was *not* going to college. But that collegiate track isn't for everyone, and the business world is replete with the stories of modern entrepreneurs who disrupted their education to launch directly into business.

Today, the younger workforce has options unimaginable to my generation. Not only is there no longer the same level of family or social shame around skipping college but many parents are encouraging summers abroad, stints with trade schools, or a focus on whatever makes their children happy and keeps them alive. Post-pandemic, with a sea change in everyone's values, happiness is sometimes the best barometer. A meteoric increase in anxiety, depression, and other mental health pressures has made many more options socially acceptable and encouraged than the traditionally prescribed paths many of us pursued.

As you reflect on your journey to date, perhaps you've been better at self-disruption than you or I give you credit for. The good news is the fear of self-disruption seems to be dissipating. Not for all, however, as many of us who are sole or primary providers for our families don't have the same flexibility—we can't be as cavalier as if we were single or financially independent. I'd suggest the main restraining forces for most of us in avoiding career self-disruption are financially related. Depending on the unemployment rate, the demand for your specific skills, and other cyclical economic issues, you stay on the shelf. But despite all these real pressures, I have to tell you that a hallmark of my own career has been firing myself.

Be Willing to Fire Yourself

I've never wanted to find myself on the receiving end of the dreaded conversation after an email invite to join my leader in a conference room we've never met in before. And, perhaps most concerningly, the human resources representative was cc'd on the email and is now sitting at the table with said boss, with a suspicious-looking manila folder resting between them. Have you been there? You take your seat, feeling the weight of the world press down on you while someone from IT dutifully cuts your access to the company servers. Yep, that moment totally sucks.

For those who haven't been through this experience and think this description feels like hyperbole, trust me, it's no exaggeration. Exits from employers are often a highly prescribed process ensuring the protection of data and the organization's reputation (no company-wide emails or Slack messages in which you denigrate your boss and organization for their obvious incompetence and moral ineptitude in letting you go). Brace yourself, as it can be a coldhearted world out there. But don't take it personally. Or, even better, prevent placing yourself in such an aggravating situation by—you guessed it—disrupting yourself first.

I know countless colleagues who I think stayed in their roles too long. Fortunately, they didn't all end up in an awkward termination meeting, but they certainly stayed below the level of their peak contribution as they embraced the safety of the status quo over self-disruption—even when the role required incrementally more from them each year. Such lack of self-disruption can become a prescription for stagnation in skill development and shrinking relevance. And despite that perception of safety, many were caught up in a downsizing as the organization went through a business transformation and their skills were less vital for the new go-to-market strategy. Did they do anything outwardly wrong? Not really. Their contributions were on par with previous years, as was their work ethic, but their skills didn't outpace the company's need for reinvention.

The lesson here is clear: you have to stay ahead of your colleagues, the marketplace, and your employer's need for reinvention and self-disruption. Yep, the most successful companies also self-disrupt as frequently as is necessary to grow and dominate.

Keep in mind the adage "Change or die." Or, if you'd like, replace "die" with "get fired," but this is a mantra that will serve you well. For companies to grow and dominate their markets, they must constantly reinvent their brands, products, services, margins, and sales strategies. They're often forced to redefine who they see as their competition and their customer. They must exercise organizational humility to ensure their products and services are meeting emerging needs and never rest on their legacy. Don't be naive; there are really only two reasons companies merge: (1) To dominate an industry or market, or (2) To create economic efficiencies internally by reducing staff and costs and ultimately returning greater profit to their shareholders. This results in jobs being eliminated, and I just want to remind you to keep your eyes and ears open so when you find yourself in this kind of situation, you're prepared. Companies disrupt themselves to grow and thrive—sometimes at the expense of valued employees. There are no sacred cows when it comes to capitalism.

To that point, you must constantly self-disrupt to be a "must-retain" associate, or be prepared when you're not seen as such to not take it personally. Self-disruption isn't only about quitting your current job to move forward. In fact, I'm not advocating that at all. Instead, learning to disrupt yourself involves a rejection of the status quo you're comfortably nestled in. This can include mindsets, relationships, skills, knowledge, patterns, emotions, surroundings, and routines. Let's take a closer look at each.

Self-Disrupt Your Mindsets

Learning to change your mind is a professional and personal competency that means you're open to being influenced. Maybe not on every topic, as you're likely not changing your religion or political affiliation—or maybe you are. But ask yourself, *As I mature and grow, am I more or less entrenched in my deeply rooted opinions?* Such opinions are often grounded and confirmed in our experiences, so consider how long it's been since you've had a novel experience that didn't challenge your current mindset. Remember the insight that many people, when they say they have twenty years of experience, have one year of experience repeated nineteen times over.

Self-Disrupt Your Relationships

As a child, I was raised to believe that loyalty to others was a fundamental quality of being a good person. Seems reasonable, which is why loyalty is one of my seven personal values I wrote about in Strategy 1. But as of late, I've seen an increase in therapists and experts proposing a new viewpoint that building healthy relationships often requires the awareness that not all people are meant to be in your life forever. Some relationships are meant to end. Sometimes the usefulness of the relationship has ended and it's best for you, and likely for them, that you both move on. Reflect on what you're doing to keep and end the right relationships for your life.

Self-Disrupt Your Skills

The most successful people have several things in common, including clarity on their values, the ability to say no to good opportunities coming at the expense of great ones, and the drive to constantly reinvent their skills, stretch their knowledge, learn new technologies, master new languages, attempt unfamiliar sports, play new games, and read books on topics that seem beyond their reach. What are you doing to shake yourself out of the status quo and learn something new?

Self-Disrupt Your Knowledge

Are you stretching your industry and business acumen beyond your comfort level and at a pace faster than your employer needs you to? Two years ago, a client offered me a large fee to keynote on "Leading During a Digital Transformation," which required me to speak for a full hour on artificial intelligence and machine learning. This was definitely outside my comfort zone, but since all things leadership are my jam, I took it on.

Truth be told, I could barely spell AI, let alone give an articulate position on it. But I immersed myself in the topic, including calling on authors, academics, and other experts, interviewing them, and eventually learning enough to crush the event. I was even rated higher by the participants than a member of the panel who was the CTO of a Fortune 50 company.

Self-Disrupt Your Patterns

I found this quote recently on social media, and I think it's fitting here: "The way you react has been repeated thousands of times, and it has become a routine for you. You are conditioned to be a certain way. And that is the challenge: to change your normal reactions, to change your routine, to take a risk and make different choices."[2] How does this apply in your life and career? Consider the way you respond to certain people with certain personalities that bother you, or how you react to feedback about your skills, behavior, or performance. The more you recognize your automatic patterns, the more likely you can assess whether they're working for or against you and for or against others. This is, in fact, an invitation to talk with those in your life and ask them to share any automatic behaviors they see in you and whether there is anything for you to act upon.

Self-Disrupt Your Emotions

Dr. Susan David, a Harvard Medical School psychologist and bestselling author of the book *Emotional Agility*, has a TED Talk that's a must-watch. Find her and absorb everything she says. She'll challenge you to consider if you, like most humans, confuse and conflate facts with opinions, emotions, and experiences. Turns out both are valuable, but facts are facts and our opinions are our opinions—and decidedly not always factual. How are you at building your self-awareness around how well you manage your emotions? Are you balancing the need to be heard and seen with recognizing that not everything you're feeling is true, helpful, or worthy of verbal expression? A profound question, I think.

Sometimes when I'm in a relationship with others, personally or professionally, and I find their behaviors, patterns, responses, and reactions are becoming frustratingly predictable, I'll think to myself, *Goodness, would you just surprise me once in my life? I'd love to be surprised by your reaction. I wish you weren't so predictable in your emotions and responses.* And I'm quite certain the same has been said or thought about me (most certainly from my wife, Stephanie).

Self-Disrupt Your Surroundings

I marvel at professionals who've lived in the same town, zip code, or area code for their entire lives. I use the word "marvel" because, even though I was brought up in a very stable family and sixty years later my mother is still living in the home I was raised in, I've since lived in twenty-two different apartments, condos, townhomes, flats, lofts, and houses. I've also owned four homes in the past six years, I change cars every two years, and I generally love new surroundings. This isn't me campaigning for you to live an itinerant life but an invitation to ask yourself if your stability in this area is a strength or a crutch.

Self-Disrupt Your Routines

Look at your habits and how you allocate and spend your time. Are there areas of refinement that, with some small, incremental changes, might be minimal self-disruptions that collectively create a new brand for you? After you read *Emotional Agility* by Susan David, pick up *Tiny Habits* by Stanford University researcher BJ Fogg. It will change how you see your own habits and the powerful impact even tiny changes can have. Then read *Atomic Habits* by James Clear, and if you haven't already, *The 7 Habits of Highly Effective People* by Stephen Covey.

There's a lot of tactical advice in this chapter, I know. So, let's sum it up like this: if you want to take intentional control over your career, determine what's holding you back. Then have the courage to self-disrupt yourself before the outside world does it for you. Because it will. It's coming.

············ EXERCISE SETUP ············

Be Willing to Disrupt Yourself

The purpose of this exercise is *not* to force an artificial or poorly timed self-disruption. Rather it's to identify what's holding you back from a well-timed and intentional self-disruption. The goal is also to ensure that when inevitable disruptions occur in the future, they're on your terms and timeline and not someone else's. You'll be asked to consider eight questions as well as your fears, limitations, passions, and motivations.

STRATEGY

Be Willing to Disrupt Yourself

Recall a time when you were EXTERNALLY disrupted by someone else.

What happened?

What was the impact?

What did I learn?

If I want to prevent this from happening again, what deliberate actions might I take now?

Recall a time when you deliberatley disrupted YOURSELF.

What happened?

What was the impact?

What did I learn?

How can I replicate this again, if wanted?

Identify your FEARS and LIMITATIONS.

FEARS	LIMITATIONS
o ______	o ______
o ______	o ______
o ______	o ______
o ______	o ______

Identify your PASSIONS and MOTIVATIONS.

PASSIONS	MOTIVATIONS
o ______	o ______
o ______	o ______
o ______	o ______
o ______	o ______

Based on my FEARS & LIMITATIONS and my PASSIONS & MOTIVATIONS, when and what will I do to deliberately disrupt myself before I'm disrupted by others?

______

______

______

______

STRATEGY

7

Take the Lead with Your Leader

I know next to nothing about Six Sigma, lean manufacturing, crypto currencies, NFTs, or ChatGPT. I can't convert Fahrenheit to Celsius in my head, tell you what the subject of physics is really about, or master a foreign language. Not my thing, people. I'll blame it on DNA.

What *is* my thing is understanding how crucial leadership is to having a great career and simultaneously how difficult it is to be a leader. I've become a bit of a pariah to many mainstream leadership authors and consultants, mainly because I hold an unpopular view of leadership regarding who should be a leader and who shouldn't. Simply put, I don't believe everyone is qualified to be a leader of people or should pursue that path (or be lured into it by their employer). Again, this isn't a common viewpoint. It's ennobling to say everyone is or can be a leader of people. It feels good and is inspiring. "Wow, even *I* can be a leader. I feel empowered already!"

I just don't believe it.

So I don't perpetuate the idea that everyone is, can, or

should be a leader of people. I guess if you parse the definition far enough, you could make a thin case that everyone contributes to the culture, positively or negatively, so they're leading in some sense. Or that most people mentor and coach others to some extent, so that's leadership. Or perhaps, in some form or fashion, because we lead projects or our own self-directed work, we're all leaders. True, I guess, from that far-reaching angle. But those examples aren't what I'm talking about. Leading yourself through a to-do list, taking your dog on their daily walk, or having a discussion with a coworker about progressing a project isn't the kind of leadership I'm concerned with.

Leaders of people interview, hire, and sometimes must fire others. They coach their teams and provide feedback and validation. They direct hard conversations around courageous topics like someone's blind spots or unconscious, negative, or self-defeating habits. They set clear, often uncomfortable expectations for their team members to stretch and grow. Leaders of people make tough decisions and nearly always lose the popularity contest among their direct reports, often people who used to be their peers and even friends—until they were promoted over them.

I don't mean to make a bigger deal out of this than is necessary, but I think it's an important point to set up this chapter. Think of it this way: not everyone is meant to be a commercial airline pilot, a patent attorney, an anesthesiologist, or a trapeze artist. In part because pilots and physicians are required to invest thousands of hours into training, pass high-stakes tests and simulations, and earn hard-won certifications or degrees. Even a trapeze certification requires six months of training and five hundred hours of non-audience practice time.[1] Leadership requires, well . . . none of that. In fact, most people become leaders accidentally, as it's the only path to promotion in most organizations.

Moving from an individual contributor role to a leader of people is too frequently how one climbing the corporate ladder earns more money, gains more influence, and wields more power. Typically, when a leadership position presents itself, the most productive and efficient individual contributor on the team gets promoted—and all the skills that served them well are now working against them as a leader of others. It's like asking the French horn player to stand up and conduct the orchestra. They are a great musician, but conducting is a totally different skill set—there's a difference between playing the notes on the page and communicating and inspiring an entire orchestra around a vision of what a piece will ultimately sound like.

But in business, we promote the French horn player to conductor all the time. The most productive nurse becomes the head of nursing; the most creative digital designer becomes the lead of the creative department; the top individual salesperson becomes the sales leader. But if my three sons are right, rarely do the top coaches in the NBA have a history of being star players.

When we pluck the top individual contributor or producer and anoint them as a leader, they're often doomed to fail—sometimes through no fault of their own. It's simply not the right career trajectory to follow while simultaneously being undertrained and underprepared for such a new role. These leadership promotions become a recipe for wreaking havoc on a team as the newly minted leader is left to lean into their existing individual contributor skill sets. Which is the *opposite* of what they should be doing.

Case Study: My Awkward Introduction to Leadership

In my own case, when I entered a leadership role I'd spent years as the top-producing sales contributor to my company's division. I consistently met my revenue goals and knew our products and services as well as or better than anyone. I was a solid sales professional who consistently met and exceeded my assigned revenue targets. This is what every sales organization craves: sales contributors generously fueling the engine of the business. I had even read Gallup's book *StrengthsFinder* and then took their CliftonStrengths assessment. My top two strengths were Competition, measuring my progress against the performance of others, and Significance, wanting to make a big impact and prioritize projects based on how much influence I have on my organization or the people around me.[2] These are superb strengths if you're a sales professional. You want your sales contributors to have a sense of competition and always be at the top of the leader board. Ensuring they feel valued, recognized, and important is key to their retention. The most poached role in every company is that of the top salespeople.

But these are *horrible* strengths in your sales leaders.

I was promoted overnight to lead seventeen of my sales peers and failed miserably out of the gate. And to make it even worse, I was selling leadership training! I was supposed to be an expert in our own services and products, all focused on how to be an effective leader, and I sucked at it—at first.

My example should illustrate two important points: first, be very deliberate about pursuing leadership roles and ensure you're set up for success with proper education and professional development. Second, consider being gentler and more forgiving to your own leader. They likely followed the same path to their position as I described above and are simply doing their best with the talent, training, and investment—or lack thereof—in their own leadership skills.

Why the second point? Look . . . let's just admit it's a popular pastime, regardless of industry or geographical location, to lament and gossip about how bad your leader is at leadership. Instead, step back and consider that leadership is a tough, thankless, and often unrelenting exercise of problem-solving day after day. I've even heard it referred to as "adult babysitting." Insulting? Sure. Accurate? Likely.

An Intentional Career Requires Taking the Lead

Remember that just because your leader is in a leadership position, it doesn't mean they have it all perfected—or even close. Just because you're the leader doesn't automatically mean you set well-crafted goals, model focus and discipline on key priorities, deliver inspiring town hall updates, or provide feedback in specific, respectful, and actionable ways.

I know CEOs of major corporations who are responsible for untold billions of revenue, tens of thousands of associates, and frightening investments into mergers and acquisitions—and they don't know jack about building culture or how stuff really gets done in their companies. Plus they often have poor interpersonal skills and are awkward at developing relationships, the very skills we all value most in our leaders. Read a complex P&L in a matter of minutes and intimately understand it? Check. Sit a key associate down face-to-face and deliver tough, factual feedback on their performance in a courageous and diplomatic way that inspires them to make a personal turnaround? Fail. There's often little correlation between being a leader and having high maturity, wisdom, knowledge, and communication skills.

This is why, as you chart the course of your own career, you need to take the lead with your leader. Just as it's your responsibility to solicit feedback from your leader, it's your responsibility, if you want an intentional career, to lead your leader—especially if they've consciously or unconsciously abdicated this responsibility themselves. Of course, I don't mean lead them in their role or responsibilities but rather in the *relationship* between the two of you. This requires moving past what you might think your subordinate role is and getting to know them better. It's likely they're privately fearful of their own potential lack of competence and, in too many cases, feel isolated and undervalued by their own leader and teams. It's a lonely life in the leadership trenches, people, and you only fully understand it when you're promoted into the position.

Taking the lead with your leader is often called "leading up." But don't confuse this with having an opinion about your leader's technical competence to do their job. Neither you nor I can take that on, and if you choose to cross that line, bring your life jacket as it rarely works out well. What I'm suggesting is analyzing how you can better understand your leader's pressures, goals, and shifting levels of self-esteem and self-confidence. They're human just like you and have fears, passions, paranoias, jealousies, and all the feelings and emotions you have—just more magnified because everyone sees theirs and talks about them. Complains about them. Amplifies and broadcasts them.

Okay, here's a small detour, but stay with me for a minute.

In my experience, the relationship in life that brings you the most joy and pain is that of your spouse or life partner.

So choose wisely. I was married comparably late in life, as I've already mentioned. (By the way, I'm convinced my three sons plot new ways every evening when the lights are out to destroy our marriage, but that's a different book.) My advice to people before getting married is to see and experience their potential spouse in every imaginable situation: a funeral, a holiday gathering with family, a professional setback, across a game table, on a long road trip, and even through the disruption of a lost friendship. Observe how your potential partner handles their finances, plans their schedule, and sets their priorities. See how they celebrate others and process someone else's wins or losses. Get a sense of their diet, passions, work ethic, and overall values in life. Analyze how they treat their parents, siblings, relatives, and every other reasonable data point you can think of as you consider likely the most consequential decision in your life.

Perfect data is impossible, but that doesn't excuse you from performing the necessary due diligence before you seal the deal. As my brother says, "In marriage, there's often an inverse correlation to the size of the diamond in the engagement ring and the longevity of the relationship." Two economic professors at Emory University have confirmed that my brother's instincts are right.[3] Even Dr. Gary Chapman, author of *The 5 Love Languages* and a guest on my podcast, will tell you "in love" wanes after about three years in most marriages.

Why this detour into investigative marital research? Because the *second* most important relationship in your life is arguably that with your leader. The fact is, most of us will spend more time awake with our work colleagues than we do with our own families.

Sorry if I've triggered any emotional PTSD by prompting you to recall the level of emotional, mental, and even physical pain professionally dysfunctional relationships have caused you. Yes, I mean physical as a manifestation of what the mental torture did to you. I occasionally pass the street of a long-ago former boss's home, and I still get physically sick to my stomach thinking about that time in my career. Listen, I'm a mature and supposedly emotionally stable adult, parent, and competent business owner, and I intentionally avoid the route past their neighborhood as the memories flood me with a concerning level of anxiety. Seems outrageous? You can find further validation from Dr. Bessel van der Kolk's book *The Body Keeps the Score: Brain, Mind, and Body in the Healing of Trauma*, which has sold two million copies, has over seventy thousand Amazon reviews, and consistently ranks in the top ten books sold *worldwide*.

Relationships cause trauma, even those with your leader. Okay, fine, *especially* those with your leader—if they're a jerk, narcissist, or sociopath, and statistically 4–12 percent of CEOs exhibit psychopathic traits similar to the 15 percent of like-minded prison inmates.[4] The problem is you get to pick your spouse/partner, but you rarely, if ever, get to pick your leader. You're stuck with them until something seismic happens and you either quit or they get fired.

Lead Your Leader to a Constructive Partnership—Not Friendship

The evidence is clear that you can't fix your leader, but you can attempt to take control of the partnership with them to build as healthy and mutually beneficial a relationship as possible. I fully recognize the numerous superb leaders out there who have had a life-changing impact on many—me included—in case you think my point of view is all leaders are jerks. Get to know your leader by completing the exercise at the end of this chapter. You'll be required to move out of your comfort zone and assess what you really know about them, and if that's enough to form a solid professional relationship—assuming they even want one.

But be careful not to make the mistake of thinking your leader is your friend. Many of us confuse friendly with friend. It's a dangerous and slippery slope and candidly an unfair and untenable situation to put your leader in. I know of a professional acquaintance who once adored their leader, and in several encounters I witnessed their praise for them. In my judgment, it was a bit much, and I could even see the leader growing uncomfortable with this person's compliments. It wasn't personally inappropriate, but it was heavy-handed in a subconsciously manipulative sense. Well, as life turns, professional disagreements occurred and the employee's expectations about what they thought should happen with their career fell short. Now the narrative from that associate about that leader is completely derogatory. Surprise, surprise!

As you run through the exercise at the end of this chapter, show prudence. Everyone has different boundaries, and if you'll forgive me for another book recommendation, check out Nedra Glover Tawwab's *Set Boundaries, Find Peace: A Guide to Reclaiming Yourself*. She was a guest on the *On Leadership with Scott Miller* podcast, and if you find her as relevant and insightful as I do, consider purchasing her more recent release, *Drama Free: A Guide to Managing Unhealthy Family Relationships*.

The relationship with your leader is vital to your mental, emotional, and even physical health. It's also a key strategy to being intentional about your career and finding more opportunities for advancement. And in case you think everything I'm suggesting is self-serving, an improved relationship with your boss benefits you both. Dr. David Rock of the NeuroLeadership Institute found that when there's mutual respect and a sense of psychological safety between manager and employee, productivity can increase by up to 20 percent. Additionally, leaders who have close professional relationships with their team members report feeling more connected to what they do, gain better insights into work processes, and have more effective meetings and conversations.[5] Not to mention the added benefit of you enjoying higher levels of job satisfaction and increased levels of engagement—all of which bodes well for the career advancement you've planned out and illustrated in Strategy 4.

Taking the lead with your leader is crucial to your promotability and organizational brand and influence. Your leader has a disproportionate voice in your career, like it or not, and you can have more impact than you may think as you become increasingly aware of their own career goals and pressures and your alignment to what they need.

Which I assure you are different from what you think.

EXERCISE SETUP

Take the Lead with Your Leader

Similar to the exercises in Strategy 3: Study Yourself and Strategy 5: Define and Build Your Brand, this exercise requires you to hold a conversation with your leader. If you're currently unemployed, you might pivot from this exercise and engage with it later. If you're a business owner or entrepreneur, you might have this conversation with a partner, investor, or client.

The purpose of this exercise is to better understand how you can "lead up" with your immediate leader—or even your leader's leader—to take better control of that relationship. When I say *control*, I don't mean in a manipulative way. Instead, I mean taking the lead by not unwittingly placing yourself in a victim role or subjecting yourself to the whims of your leader, which may adversely affect you over time.

Understand the Human Side

Create a mindset where you think of your leader less formally and more as a human being. Identify what you know about them as you work to answer the Getting to Know Your Leader questions accurately. This isn't license for a fishing or snooping expedition; rather, it's a chance for you to reflect on your leader's complete self and their professional journey. Write down their fears, goals, passions, and pressures, because the better you understand your leader, the more effectively you can take the lead in your relationship with them. I don't recommend you necessarily interview them for this specific information, however, but draw on what you know—and think you know—from your experiences with them.

Use the Leader Conversation Starter

When you engage in the conversation with your leader, it can be formal or casual. The decision is up to you, based on the rapport and overall level of trust in your relationship. Decide which format or venue is best for this meeting and use the Leader Conversation Starter to prepare. The Leader Conversation Starter should educate and empower you to relate to and connect with your leader. The more you understand their career journey, the specific pressures they're facing, and how you can help them achieve their own goals, the more inclined they'll be to include you in their journey.

Through all ten strategies and related exercises in this book, carefully determine how often you choose to engage with your direct leader. If you involve them in too many exercises, it could become fatiguing for them and even undermine some of your goals. Assess your relationship with them and act accordingly.

Take the Lead with Your Leader

GETTING TO KNOW YOUR LEADER

Answer these questions about your current leader on your own. This is not intended to be an interview.

Q: *What are the major milestones of their career?*

A:

Q: *What is their relationship like with their leader?*

A:

Q: *What are their key strengths/areas of confidence?*

A:

Q: *What are their weaknesses/insecurities?*

A:

Q: *What success would they need to achieve to earn a promotion?*

A:

Q: *What pressures are they under that, if you knew about, would make you more relevant?*

A:

Q: *What fears might they have that contribute to their professional stress?*

A:

Q: *What passion do they have that might ignite their own career?*

A:

Q: *What challenges do they face in leading the team?*

A:

Q: *What improvements in my own performance could benefit them?*

A:

LEADER CONVERSATION STARTER

Use this tool to facilitate a strategic conversation with your leader.

Q: *What are your most pressing short-term needs?*

A:

Q: *What are your most vital long-term strategic needs?*

A:

Q: *What part of your role has changed that I should better understand?*

A:

Q: *Are there specific goals you're trying to achieve that you feel are out of reach for our team?*

A:

Q: *What frustrations are you facing that could be resolved if I/our team knew of them?*

A:

Q: *What one thing do you need to accomplish to build your influence beyond your current commitments?*

A:

Q: *What pressures are you facing from your leader(s) that I/our team can help with?*

A:

Write your own questions here:

Q:

A:

Q:

A:

Q:

A:

STRATEGY

8

Do the Job You Were Hired For, Plus the One You Want

Doing the job you were hired for, plus the one you want, is a key strategy for planning and realizing an intentional career. The benefit comes from finding a way to bridge your current responsibilities with where you'd like to progress to next. It not only proves what you're capable of but gives you a head start in growing from your current responsibilities to those reflective of the next milestone of your career plan. But because such a balancing act can be tricky, allow me to spend the bulk of this chapter unpacking the pitfalls around doing both the job you were hired for and the one you want—and how to avoid them. We'll look at:

- Being out of sync with your leader.
- Focusing too much on the wrong job.
- Not treading carefully and wisely.
- Relying on hope rather than building the support of your leader.

Pitfall 1: Being Out of Sync with Your Leader

With some regularity in my leadership career, when I was serving in the C-suite, a more junior colleague from a different division would approach me for some career advice. When I say "with some regularity," I mean this would happen frequently. It was evidence that, despite the many perceived downsides related to my brand, one clear upside was that associates across the company viewed me as very strategic with my own career. I had gained a reputation for being one of, if not the best, leaders to grow your career under.

The themes around such meetings were generally the same—an associate wanted to move up the career ladder while increasing their income, and they were debating whether to stay inside the company or go elsewhere. Without fail, they'd put considerable thought into their next steps. Some had begun searching for roles outside the organization and had even begun the interviewing process. Others had their eyes set on a specific role inside the company, usually quite ambitious in my estimation. It never ceased to surprise me how many people wanted to become a vice president and truly thought they deserved it. I don't recall agreeing with any of them, knowing what it took to earn that designation and responsibility, but I digress.

After these associates had heartfelt conversations with me about their dilemma, I'd ask two questions. Remember, this happened dozens of times. I'd hold essentially the same conversation and ask the same two questions.

Question 1: "What are your professional values?" Of course, none of them even knew what I was talking about let alone carefully thought through and identified their values.

I'd patiently listen to a stream of quickly spouted ideas before encouraging them to take the necessary time to delve deeper. My first advice was in the form of a little pressure to think about their values more carefully and solidify what they were on their own time. Nearly all of them would return later and talk about how valuable the conversation and exercise had been for them, which is precisely the reason I made it the first chapter in this book. Yes, that means if you've made it this far *without* having gone through that foundational and essential career exercise, let me suggest you go back and make that critical investment in yourself—sooner rather than later.

Question 2: "How would your current leader rate your performance?" Without exception, everyone would tell me how they were crushing their current job, and how they were certain their leader was very pleased with their contribution. Most said they would receive a glowing review and were most concerned that their leader wouldn't champion them for a promotion because they wouldn't want to lose them from their current role and team.

Lovely.

But also delusional.

I made it a habit to press this issue with them and really probe as to their track record. If they were in sales, I asked about meeting their quarterly revenue goals. If they were in marketing, finance, or product development, I delved into their respective deliverables and MBOs (management by objectives). I asked about past and recent reviews and if they'd ever been on a performance plan. Again, the responses were always positive—glowing, even—about their view of how their current leader saw their performance.

At the next opportunity, I would deftly and intentionally place myself in a position to encounter said gushing leader—perhaps in the lunchroom or at a company event, or a chance encounter caused by me loitering around their office area (seeing that now in print, yeah, it seems a little creepy). But you get the point: I made a deliberate attempt for a "chance encounter" where I could turn a normal conversation into a question about the associate's performance without raising any red flags. On further reflection, maybe I was crazy for putting that much work into someone simply asking me for career advice. But then again, maybe that's the reason people came to me for that advice in the first place.

Anyway, once I'd ducked out from behind the office fern and caught the leader's attention, I'd say something like, "Hey, congrats on the traction your app is getting in Asia. You've really assembled a superb team." They would thank me, of course. After all, who doesn't like a compliment—especially when it's true. That would give me my doorway into the real purpose of our conversation.

"I think [insert associate's name here] was on that project, right? They seem like a valuable contributor—you pleased with their performance?" Now, this might seem a little off to many people, but since the question came from an executive officer in the firm, nobody suspected I had a motive other than just general interest in all associates and their contributions. I was always careful not to divulge any confidences with the team member during my sleuthing.

You'd think after the glowing report I'd heard from the associate that their leader would start offering praise. But *inevitably* their answer was some kind of guttural groan followed by, "Why are you asking? You want to bring them over to your team?" And before I could come up with a reply, they'd quickly follow with, "Because you can have them. How fast do you need the transition to be?"

That wasn't the *exact* language used every time, but it was most certainly the sentiment—said supposed-to-be-gushing leader zeroing in on the fact that I was asking about someone on their team and not only inviting me to proceed with possible recruitment but practically holding the door open and pushing the associate through it. Once I assured them I wasn't on a fishing expedition for potential new team members, the leader would nod as if they recognized I knew the same things about the associate they did. Then they'd follow up with a litany of issues around that associate's performance, self-awareness, and maturity. Not a trashing but a dramatically different narrative than what the associate had portrayed to me. "Chelsea has only made three of her last seven quarters and is on track to miss again. . . . Zach is a great guy and I really like him as a person, but he seems incapable of prioritizing his projects, so his deliverables are late. . . . Luiz just takes longer than anyone else on the team to figure things out, and it slows everyone else down."

There are several insights to unpack from this series of occurrences. First, shame on the leader for allowing any confusion about how they viewed that team member's performance. Allowing any dissonance between their reality and that of their direct report is blatantly poor leadership. Second, shame on the employee for either disregarding the feedback they had received or obfuscating it when speaking with me and, more importantly, not taking the lead with their leader to ensure their feedback sessions were happening at the right cadence and with the right levels of effectiveness.

The big idea for you to take away is this: *a gap will always exist between how you think your leader views your performance and how they actually view it.* I know, you think you're the exception—just like every associate who came seeking my advice assumed *they* were the exception. They weren't, and neither are you.

Welcome to human interactions.

The psychology explaining such gaps is rooted in our individual levels of self-esteem and confidence. Self-esteem is defined as the subjective judgment we make about our own worth and capabilities, while confidence is the belief that we will succeed in a particular venture or accomplishment. When we have higher levels of self-esteem and confidence, we're at risk to believe we can do more than we can or than what our leaders have experienced or believe as well. Which isn't to say self-esteem and confidence are bad; like most things in life, what surfaces as a strength, if overplayed, can quickly become a weakness.

Notice that my career advice in this book is focused on *self-awareness* and not *self-esteem* per se. Self-esteem is important, sure. And research suggests having a clear vision of your future career path (Strategy 4) can provide motivation, direction, and focus that can boost your overall self-confidence.[1] Just take this experience as a cautionary tale: judiciously keep an eye on how your successes—perceived or real—and your innate sense of self-confidence may show up in ways that are out of sync with your leader's perspective. It's your responsibility, as uncomfortable and incredulous as it may be, to get into sync and narrow any gaps as much as possible. As illuminated in Strategy 7: Take the Lead with Your Leader, you will almost certainly need to step up more than you think you should to ensure you're both on the same page.

Pitfall 2: Focusing Too Much on the Wrong Job

My experience has shown that often the dissonance on the topic of performance isn't so much that the employee isn't doing a great job but rather because they're doing the *wrong* job. They're frequently too focused on the part of their job that invigorates them, brings them significance, and provides satisfaction. It's completely understandable that if you're in sales you may like maintaining existing client relationships better than you like prospecting for new business. Or, if you're in R&D, I'm guessing for some the D is much more fun and rewarding than the R, as it would be for me.

The point is, we gravitate to those areas of our jobs that bring us validation. Often those areas are *not* the ones our leaders value—or think they hired us for. Certainly, every role has a hierarchy of important responsibilities. In this book, I reference sales examples frequently because most of my career was spent in sales, and regardless of the organization, not much happens and not many get paid until someone actually sells something.

If you're in a sales position, you need to make hitting your own assigned and agreed-upon revenue targets your all-consuming obsession. Not offering feedback on how the products could be improved. Not coaching other sales colleagues on how to be more consultative. Not offering to revamp the entire website. You have one primary job: hit and ideally exceed your quota, every month. Every quarter. Every year. This is how you build a reputation as someone who is trusted, is respected, and understands prioritization. You also don't want to be so obsessed with only hitting your sales targets that your brand becomes one who is self-serving and unwilling to contribute to anything beyond your own commission. Without question, the salesperson who hits all their targets will have elevated influence on those concerns and issues I just listed. And conversely, the sales associate who rarely delivers on their assigned goal will just be viewed as a gadfly highlighting excuses for their lack of performance.

Like every role in life, it's all about balance. Having fierce clarity on your top goal and letting nothing come at its expense must be simultaneously balanced with an awareness that more may be asked of you. You need to decide how you will address that.

This example can be extrapolated into every career. If you're a dental hygienist, your main job is likely a flawless teeth cleaning so the dentist can come in and do their job in minimal time without having to backtrack over your work because you were distracted by talking to your patient about their next vacation—which is likely part of your job in terms of patient service and building relationships and referrals. If you're the front desk representative at a hotel, and you're solving every guest issue that pops up to the chagrin of the long line of grumpy guests waiting to check in, that's going to be your brand: slow check-in.

Pitfall 3: Not Treading Carefully and Wisely

In every role throughout your career, you'll need to learn and perfect the balance between doing the job you have—the one you were hired for—and the one you want. Well-intended and super ambitious climbers (that would be me) set their sights on the next role in their multidecade plan, taking the initiative to volunteer for new assignments typically associated with that higher position. This is generally a great strategy when done carefully and wisely. Run through this checklist before you take on new responsibilities tied to the role or job you want:

- You have complete confidence and objective feedback that you're delivering on your current responsibilities at a level indicating you can reasonably take on more.
- You've talked with your leader and have certainty that they share the same opinion of your performance as you do.
- You continuously self-assess as to whether any new stretch duties are in any way competing against your brand or working against you in terms of your current responsibilities. Others will likely see this long before you do, so solicit their feedback.
- You've appropriately asked for permission to take on more instead of simply feeling empowered to do so. Depending on the culture of your organization, tolerance for such self-empowerment can vary dramatically, so make sure you're in sync.
- You've ensured the new responsibilities you're assuming aren't perceived as someone else's job. That would likely be the quickest way to be viewed as an opportunist and branded as a pariah.

Pitfall 4: Relying on Hope Rather Than Building the Support of Your Leader

It's vital that your current leader reinforces your view of your current performance and becomes your unrelenting champion and supporter. The vast majority of the time, upward movement within an organization will require your current leader to sign off on any release of you in your current role. They'll also be crucial as a reference for you to their hiring peer. Don't underestimate how important it is for you to strategically manage this process rather than just hope it all works out in your favor. It's a poor career strategy to assume your leader will take on the heart of an angel and suddenly check all their grievances about you when asked for their honest and genuine recommendation. Your leader will not, out of kindness, simply ignore everything but your strengths. Even if they *want* to get rid of you, smart leaders recognize that a recommendation puts their own reputation and brand on the line as well.

Remember that hope isn't a strategy.

Let me elaborate. I once worked with a very competent colleague who was contagiously positive and a delight to be around. She would often tell me, in tense moments of high-stakes results, "Scott, relax; it will all work out." And as much as I liked her, it incensed me that she thought stuff would just all work itself out. That's not how life goes. You have to *work it out* for it to *all work out*.

Early in my sales career, an international assignment came up in the company. It was a year-long stint in the United Kingdom, and I wanted it worse than I wanted the motor scooter my parents never bought me in junior high school and significantly worse than I wanted that tennis ball machine in elementary school my parents also never bought me. I now own multiple scooters and will absolutely be buying a tennis ball machine just for personal edification. (Yes, my adult life is fixated on solving all the injustices my parents inflicted upon me in my youth.)

The position was a stretch for me in many ways and wasn't a role posted on the internal job board. It was more of an assignment than a permanent job, but I knew I could make it work if I was just given a chance. Candidly, this was a plumb assignment as it came with an expat compensation plan—meaning they adjusted your income for the local living expenses, paid your rent, gave you a car, and flew you back and forth to the States with reasonable considerations. What I didn't understand was that the UK business was in some turmoil, and executive leadership had been watching my performance for a few years as an individual sales contributor. I'd been delivering on my monthly sales commitments, month after month, with intense ownership. The senior vice president charged with turning that UK business unit around, who I knew of but had no relationship with, came to my leader and asked if he thought I'd be a good candidate. At this point they were close friends, and even though my boss reported to him, they greatly trusted each other's counsel. My leader could have ruined this for me in one sentence.

He didn't.

He sang my praises. And I'm sure he shared lots of watchouts as well. I've got my own crazy, just like you do.

But simply put, my boss landed this role for me. Period. It benefited him in no way personally or professionally. In fact, it put him in a huge bind, as I'd grown to be the division's top revenue producer and he had no backup plan for me leaving. That meant there was every reason for him to encourage his friend to pass me over and look elsewhere. But because I'd managed my relationship with him so intentionally over the years—even through the ups and downs—he was willing to put my best interests ahead of his own. Yes, I had hoped I would get the position. But I didn't stop there. I had also built a brand and reputation for success and had carefully managed the relationship with my leader along the way.

I moved to the UK for a year, where I apparently crushed it, because my next ten years in the company were a meteoric rise. When I returned to corporate headquarters a year later, I was promoted to be a sales manager, director, general manager, vice president, and soon thereafter, an executive vice president and chief marketing officer—every position illustrated on my long-term plan, executed with precision.

My path may not be your desired path, but the principles are universal. I truly believe the pivot in my entire career was landing this foreign assignment, and it only happened because of how my then-leader, Chuck Farnsworth, positioned me for the role with his own leader. I'd given him the reason to do so by simply and maniacally doing the job I was hired for so that I could then do the job I wanted.

EXERCISE SETUP

Do the Job You Were Hired For, Plus the One You Want

I'd like to provide clarity on a question I often hear: Should the two pieces of this strategy happen concurrently, or in a one-two sequence?

The answer depends on your specific situation. The higher your self-awareness and accuracy about how well you're perceived at delivering on the job you were hired for (the one you're currently in and need to be consistently crushing), the better you'll be set up to also do the one you want in the future. The most common mistake I see is associates having a delusional perspective on their current performance and irresponsibly taking on new tasks that they think will set them up for a future promotion. But instead, this strategy has the opposite effect. Not only do they lose earning the future role but they sometimes actually lose their current role. You need to bring a hyperaccurate self-assessment to your unique situation and govern yourself accordingly.

Do the Job You Were Hired For

This is "duh" advice for us all. But it's surprising how often we become unintentionally complacent in our performance, and as a result, our brands suffer. How we view our own performance is often shockingly different from how our leader views it. Closing this gap should be an obsession. Get real with yourself. Truthfully rate your performance on a scale of 1 to 10 using the questions on the left side of pp. 182–83. Then ask your leader to do so using the same questions. Compare answers, then get to work to ensure any gaps are closed or sufficiently aligned.

Focus on Doing the Job You Want

Only when your leader and you are congruent about the quality of your performance should you begin progressing toward the job you want.

At the end of the worksheet, identify the tasks, projects, or other duties you want to proactively take on to achieve any future job title or role on your long-term plan. Here's the big idea: resist the lure of accomplishing projects and wins for a future role if your current performance isn't best in class.

STRATEGY 8

Do the Job You Were Hired For, Plus the One You Want

THE JOB I WAS HIRED FOR

Only when you and your leader agree on the quality of your current job performance can you begin to work on the job you want.

MY POINT OF VIEW

LOW — **HIGH**

1. *My ability to focus on what my leader needs from me*

①—②—③—④—⑤—⑥—⑦—⑧—⑨—⑩

2. *My ability to determine and elevate priorities*

①—②—③—④—⑤—⑥—⑦—⑧—⑨—⑩

3. *My ability to focus on timely deliverables*

①—②—③—④—⑤—⑥—⑦—⑧—⑨—⑩

MY LEADER'S POINT OF VIEW

LOW — **HIGH**

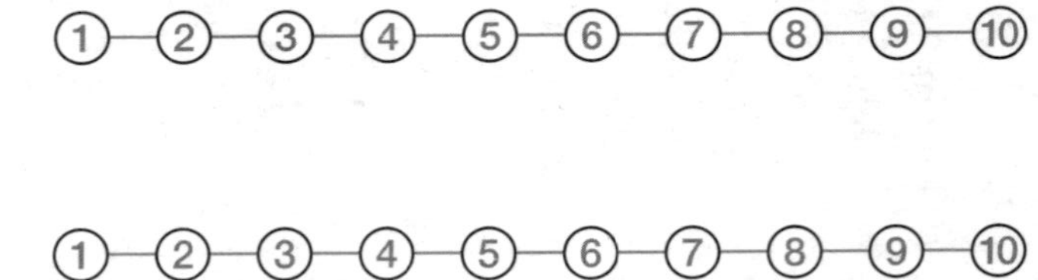

①—②—③—④—⑤—⑥—⑦—⑧—⑨—⑩

①—②—③—④—⑤—⑥—⑦—⑧—⑨—⑩

①—②—③—④—⑤—⑥—⑦—⑧—⑨—⑩

MY POINT OF VIEW		MY LEADER'S POINT OF VIEW	
LOW	HIGH	LOW	HIGH

4. *My ability to achieve mutually agreed-upon goals*

My point of view	My leader's point of view
1 — 2 — 3 — 4 — 5 — 6 — 7 — 8 — 9 — 10	1 — 2 — 3 — 4 — 5 — 6 — 7 — 8 — 9 — 10

5. *My ability to receive and act on feedback*

My point of view	My leader's point of view
1 — 2 — 3 — 4 — 5 — 6 — 7 — 8 — 9 — 10	1 — 2 — 3 — 4 — 5 — 6 — 7 — 8 — 9 — 10

6. *My ability to minimize drama*

My point of view	My leader's point of view
1 — 2 — 3 — 4 — 5 — 6 — 7 — 8 — 9 — 10	1 — 2 — 3 — 4 — 5 — 6 — 7 — 8 — 9 — 10

7. *My ability to build and not diminish the culture*

My point of view	My leader's point of view
1 — 2 — 3 — 4 — 5 — 6 — 7 — 8 — 9 — 10	1 — 2 — 3 — 4 — 5 — 6 — 7 — 8 — 9 — 10

8. *My overall performance*

My point of view	My leader's point of view
1 — 2 — 3 — 4 — 5 — 6 — 7 — 8 — 9 — 10	1 — 2 — 3 — 4 — 5 — 6 — 7 — 8 — 9 — 10

THE JOB I WANT

1. *Identify the next job title or role on your long-term plan.*

____

2. *List the projects or responsibilities you could proactively offer to help on—or boldly take over—that will build others' confidence that you're ready for a promotion.*

____

____

____

____

____

____

____

____

____

____

____

____

____

Common watch-outs to look for:

Do not, under any circumstances, begin applying this side of the worksheet unless you are in complete congruence with your leader about your job performance and they have validated that you are crushing your current role.

Be careful not to tread on other people's responsibilities. You want your brand to be "helpful and strategic," not "opportunistic."

Deliberately select those projects or responsibilities that add value and are not currently being fulfilled by someone else.

This exercise assumes that your next role will be in your current organization. If it's not, you may choose to begin building the skills needed to assume your future role.

STRATEGY

9

Keep Your Ear to the Ground

Building networks, keeping your eyes and ears open, and gathering intel are crucial to having a deliberate and intentional career. Or, as I've termed it, keeping your ear to the ground. Keeping your ear to the ground means ensuring you're aware of and aligned with any organizational knowledge that can best position your own career growth—while staying far away from what amounts to company gossip. This is important, because one of the first temptations you'll face in keeping your ear to the ground will be to further traffic in such gossip instead of simply assessing, and, if warranted, acting on any relevant information.

The Temptation to Turn Information into Gossip

Don't underestimate how damaging being a gossip can be to your brand and career. I assure you, if I were to poll one thousand CEOs, chief human resource officers, or other C-suite executives and ask them, "What is the biggest cultural problem in your organization?" The vast majority would name gossip.

Simply put, gossip is the biggest cancer inside every company. The issue is, no one admits to participating in it. It's always "someone else doing it." Never you. The fact is all of us engage in some level of gossip—consciously and unconsciously. And when we do, we find some way to justify it. Let me state this very boldly: you want your brand to be as far away from trafficking in gossip as is emotionally, mentally, and physically possible. This strategy is about gaining access to actionable and appropriate information so you can create a more intentional career. This strategy is not about manipulating, conniving, or positioning yourself to gain access to inappropriate information that allows you to leapfrog over someone or capitalize on someone's unfortunate situation.

I know it may be tempting to think that some amount of gossip is simply a fact of life, personally and professionally, and that not much can be done about it. As a rebuttal, let me share a powerful example that shows the difference one person can make when it comes to gossip.

The Power of One

For more than a decade of my career, I reported directly to the CEO, which can be überstressful. The CEO was a truly remarkable person. He checked every box, and even double-checked most of them.

- Ivy League education
- Unimpeachable integrity
- Relentless work ethic

- Impeccably dressed and groomed
- Extremely physically healthy (summited the Matterhorn, participated in over twenty Kona IRONMANs, and so on)
- Extraordinarily well-read and well-traveled
- Unrelatable personal wealth
- Forty-plus-year marriage
- Lockbox with confidences
- Sophisticated taste and social manners
- Visionary, inspiring, kind, humble
- Rigorous thinker
- Dedicated to his faith
- Personal discipline like nobody I've ever met

IT WAS EXHAUSTING.

Trying to keep up with him? Impossible.

Trying to please him? Doubly impossible.

In a moment of insanity, I shared with him that it would be really difficult to be his son. Seriously, I told this to the CEO on Father's Day weekend. Kiss those stock options goodbye! His standards were unrelenting and consequently could be very diminishing to a person's self-esteem and self-confidence. I don't think for a moment he meant to minimize anyone. He just wasn't willing to lower his own standards to accommodate someone else's lesser standards. Ever.

Of all his superb traits listed above, the one I most admired was his zero tolerance for gossip. From himself as CEO and from all who reported to him. He set the standard for all of us with his own behavior. Whenever there was an executive team meeting and someone missed it, he would table any discussion that related to their projects. He simply didn't want other people attempting to represent the opinions of the absent team member. He was known for saying, "I see Scott's missing today. What time does his plane land in Atlanta? 3:30? Great. Let's move to another topic, and when he lands he can dial in and represent his position." He never allowed other people to characterize someone else in case they might do so poorly, intentionally or not. He fully understood that, as humans, we all have hidden agendas and less-than-noble strategies that are often meant to advance our own self-interests.

Also known as gossip.

As psychiatrist and neuroscientist Dr. Daniel Amen, a frequent guest on the *On Leadership* podcast, once said to me, "Everyone is out for themselves. Some of us are just better at hiding it than others."

Bam!

Not only did the CEO not engage in gossip but he didn't tolerate it among others. Whenever someone might share a frustration about another colleague or team member, he'd immediately ask if they'd shared their thoughts directly with that person. Obviously, the answer was frequently no, and so he'd immediately encourage them to do so. His lack of tolerance for any level of duplicity became the company norm. Having one person at the top consistently modeling that behavior meant it spread like wildfire. As a result, the company was one of the most gossip-free organizations I've ever worked in or consulted for.

All because of one person's modeling.

But it's easier writing about it than practicing it in real

life. We find gossip at nearly every turn, including houses of worship, schools, recreation centers, and our own homes. Despite its abundance, I've met very few people in life who admit to being a gossip. I think we'd agree, there is no prize awarded for confessing to being one.

And then there's me. I can't keep a secret to save my life. If it's a matter of legality, which sometimes is the case in a public company, then I will rise to the occasion. But beyond that, telling me something means telling the world—which, as I've already admitted, is lamentably part of my brand. Likely it's due to a combination of me wanting to feel important and look as if I'm in the know, having a lack of impulse control, and generally showing poor judgment when it comes to keeping secrets.

So here are the big ideas thus far. First, I wrote this chapter for me as much as for you. You think *not* trafficking in gossip is easy? I struggle with it all the time, and yet I know it can have dire consequences. Though I haven't and won't share anything that could be detrimental to the organization, those little tidbits about so-and-so around the water cooler are another matter. I'm willing to step up to a greater degree of accountability in this regard and invite you to do the same.

Second, don't underestimate the power one person's example can have. Sure, the actions of a CEO carry a lot of weight, but we humans are nothing if not constant observers of each other. If you want your brand to be someone who keeps confidences and doesn't ever traffic in gossip, whether you're in the C-suite or not, model that behavior until it becomes so well understood that someone shares a similar story about you that I have about my former boss.

Finding Balance in the Middle

There's a fine line between trafficking in gossip and acting on relevant and valuable information. But this can often be subjective, expressed in adages like "One person's trash is another person's treasure" or "One person's terrorist is another person's freedom fighter." It's up to you to understand the difference between being a gossip and being in the know to help progress your career. After all, organizations are merely collections of people all trying to get stuff done together, and we know how challenging that can be.

I've always been a bit shocked at how far apart the two extremes seem to be for most professionals. On one hand—let's visualize the far left end of a horizontal continuum—is the person branded as a company gossip. They know everything—who's getting fired, hired, and promoted. They know who's having the affair and who's about to quit. They somehow know about the next acquisition or divestiture, or at least they say they did when it's announced. They know which jobs are opening next, which leaders are the best to work for, and if the newest job posted really has approved funding behind it or not. They also traffic in this information for their own status and political benefit. (And yes, I've just basically described all 435 elected members of the United States House of Representatives.)

These people use information as currency in their organization and barter with it, and even build power from it. "I know something you don't know" would be their theme song. Sad but true, as over 90 percent of congressional members get reelected each term.

I can recall an associate who was remarkably talented, perhaps one of the most technically talented people I've ever worked with. Her ability to process information rapidly could be quite intimidating. She deftly understood most technologies, asked piercingly insightful questions, and easily got to the root cause of an issue. She was profoundly talented.

And a complete gossip.

Totally untrustworthy, in my opinion, and I stayed as far from her as politically, culturally, and even physically possible. In short, I found that her lack of trustworthiness totally eclipsed her talent—at least with me. I would never hire her or recommend anyone else hire her either. Quite shrewdly, she would get people to open up, share, confess, and divulge. And she was a master at using that information to align with risers and malign those she didn't like or respect.

Now visualize the absolute opposite end of the continuum. On this far right side is the ostrich, content with burying their head in the sand. Such office ostriches are so deeply immersed in their work, their small world, and their own issues and concerns that they have zero clue what's going on one cubicle over, let alone one building over. They generally tend to be somewhat naive, and perhaps the "ignorance is bliss" strategy works well enough for them. Mind you, these are the same people who are absolutely shocked when there's a layoff, acquisition, or some high-level termination or exit.

If you can't guess, that place you want to be is in the middle. And it's up to you to define what that looks, sounds, and feels like. I can't tell you the right balance, as it's different for each individual career and work culture.

Putting Your Ear to the Ground Best Practices

Putting your ear to the ground means gaining a solid understanding of the facts and the strategic direction of your team, division, or broader organization. Having a keen eye on the changing landscape of your industry and how it affects your goals can help you navigate new and unplanned opportunities that present themselves over the course of your career. Pay attention to any changes in areas such as industry trends, market dynamics, customer demand, technology advancements—and how your organization plans to adapt, pivot, or otherwise address these. Look at your own professional development and attend courses, conferences, or seminars. Take advantage of the resources I've assembled for you in the bonus strategy, Own Your Development, to gain further insights into what the lay of the land might be.

In addition, I encourage you to identify up to six people inside your organization you can talk to about these issues. They should be people you trust who are well respected and, in most cases, more senior than you. I call these people *influencers*—and you're on a fact-finding mission, not a treasure hunt. These six individuals may or may not be part of the Team of Eight you assembled in Strategy 3 or the three people you learned from in Strategy 5. It's your decision who to add to this list, but here's the criteria: pick people who can help you understand the direction and momentum of the organization and shine a light on areas of potential confusion or clarity for you—but who aren't known as gossips themselves.

Questions to Consider

Use this list of questions to prompt conversations with those who might provide helpful insights and information about your organization.

- Can you share the overall financial health of our organization?
- What are the top priorities of the organization?
- How can someone at my level connect to the top priorities?
- Who are the best leaders to work for to earn a promotion?
- What behaviors are most respected and valued here?
- Why do some people stagnate here?
- What's no longer valued here?
- What technical and interpersonal skills are valued here?
- Which divisions in the organization are the most progressive?

Watch-Outs

In addition to resisting the temptation to traffic in gossip, use these reminders as watch-outs with those you engage in with "ear to the ground" conversations.

- Be mindful of your brand. Don't ask prying or sensitive questions.
- Keep your questions related to the business.

- Resist asking questions you're not in a position to know the answers to.
- Ask open-ended questions.
- State your intent. Be transparent about why you're asking.
- Resist pressing for more information if you feel the person is uncomfortable.
- Thank them for their insights.
- Don't divulge information that might be overshared.
- Above all, earn their trust by keeping confidences.

Post-Pandemic Considerations

A final point worth bringing up is that keeping your ear to the ground has become more difficult post-pandemic. The ground is gone. Literally. Depending on where your organization landed on policies about physical, hybrid, or even fully virtual work, it can feel like it's nearly impossible to know what's going on organization-wide.

Part of your challenge is to determine who has access to accurate and actionable information on the present and future. Where is the company truly headed? Who is rising and consolidating influence? Which projects, products, and services are worth aligning with or working on? What only seems vital versus what really is? It's difficult to advise you specifically around this because of the company nuances at play. But you should build a strategy of how you plan to navigate your increasingly virtual environment so you're not left in the dark, able to only guess about what's happening.

EXERCISE SETUP

Keep Your Ear to the Ground

This is a simple yet valuable exercise that can easily go sideways if your intent isn't pure or transparent. Keeping your ear to the ground is not exclusively about "being in the know" or becoming your company's mobile water cooler. That's called gossip, and you want to distance yourself from it completely. Gossip is a cancer in every organization, and you should have nothing to do with it.

I've replicated the "watch-outs" on the right side of the worksheet to help prevent you from going sideways or appearing to ask questions that aren't appropriate, as well as the "questions to consider" on the left side. Keep in mind this is an evergreen, ongoing exercise that you should repeat as needed. Mix and match questions or add your own, depending on whom you've identified as an influencer. The key is to state your intent with each person and ask questions that can help you better understand the landscape of the organization, which will help you make intentional decisions about your next career move.

STRATEGY

Keep Your Ear to the Ground

Questions to consider:

Can you share the overall financial health of our organization?

What are the top priorities of the organization?

How can someone at my level connect to the top priorities?

Who is/are the best leader(s) to work for to earn a promotion?

What behaviors are most respected/valued here?

Why do some people stagnate here?

What's no longer valued?

What technical/interpersonal skills are valued?

Which divisions in the organization are most valuable?

____

____

____

Add your own questions here

Influencers in Your Organization

NAME / ROLE

1

- ________________
- ________________
- ________________
- ________________
- ________________
- ________________

NAME / ROLE

2

- ________________
- ________________
- ________________
- ________________
- ________________
- ________________

NAME / ROLE

3

Common watch-outs to look for:

Be mindful of your brand.

Don't ask prying or sensitive questions.

Keep your questions related to the business.

Resist asking questions that you're not in a position to know the answer.

Ask open-ended questions.

State your intent. Be transparent about why you're asking.

Resist pressing for more information if you feel the person is uncomfortable.

Thank them for their insights.

Don't divulge information that might be overshared.

Above all, earn their trust by keeping confidences.

Add your own watch-outs here

Influencers in Your Organization

NAME / ROLE

4

NAME / ROLE

5

NAME / ROLE

6

STRATEGY

Dig Your Well Before You're Thirsty

Famous author, columnist, and speaker Harvey Mackay wrote many books, including *Dig Your Well Before You're Thirsty: The Only Networking Book You'll Ever Need.* I've named this final chapter in tribute to his book, as I find the main concept to be a common dilemma many professionals face. They become complacent in building their professional network outside of their current organization. If and when they leave abruptly (usually due to termination), they find themselves with a shallow well of contacts because they've invested the majority of their networking time inside their current company to accomplish the projects and goals they've been tasked with. The people you work with now are not likely to be the same ones who will help you find employment outside of that organization. You need to build a robust network both inside and outside of your current employer.

Invest in Your Network (Not Your Résumé)

Before the *On Leadership with Scott Miller* podcast truly took off, I hosted a weekly radio program on iHeart radio called *Great Life, Great Career with Scott Miller*. This was an hour-long interview program where, similar to the weekly podcasts I host now, I curated interesting and valuable guests. One radio interview featured an executive recruiter, Lindsay Landsberg, who was based out of Chicago. She shared some information with me I'll never forget: more than 80 percent of all jobs are filled through a referral.

Let that just marinate with you for a few moments.

There are two kinds of professionals when it comes to career advancement: those who have a résumé and those who have a network. Another way to express this is, "It's not what you know, but who you know."

Have you sufficiently dug your networking well? *Before* you get thirsty?

Let me ask a few questions to level set:

- What is your network like inside of your current employer? Is it just those in your division, floor, building, or campus?
- What was your network like with your previous employers or companies? Do you keep it warm, or did you drop them all cold as soon as you left?
- How robust is your social network, meaning people you know in some other way than through your employer? Regardless of whether you're an introvert, extrovert, or no vert whatsoever, are you building and nurturing relationships through your local restaurants,

house of worship, country clubs, recreation centers, and gym? How about every vendor you've ever hired, relatives, friends of friends, and that person you sat next to at last summer's outdoor music festival?

- Are you making use of your social media connections? LinkedIn allows for thirty thousand connections. If you have any less than that, what are you waiting for? You can have an unlimited number of followers (all connections are followers, but not all followers are connections). How about Facebook, X (Twitter), Instagram, YouTube, TikTok, and any new channels that have emerged since I wrote these words?
- How robust is your contribution to your social media platforms? Are you just a spectator, or do you contribute value to your network? Have you set aside daily or weekly designated time to build and maintain your social media connections? Digging your well before you're thirsty does, in fact, require some digging.

Dig in New Ground

About three years before I announced my departure from FranklinCovey, I had an epiphany. I realized that as a result of moving into the C-suite seven years earlier, the time I spent in the CEO's office in meetings and physically in the division I was leading added up to 100 percent of my time and attention. I was no longer out visiting with clients, attending conferences, or in any way building a network outside the company. I was exceptionally well networked inside the company, but with only twelve hundred people worldwide, I wasn't exactly digging a deep well.

No offense to all my colleagues, but few to none of them were going to help me find what was next for me. I had an eye-opening experience one day when I came to realize, *I'm fifty and am the CMO of a global, public company, and after twenty-five years in this organization, I know hardly anyone outside the firm. I need to change that. Immediately!*

And so I did. I intentionally started building my social platforms. I started speaking at more conferences and traveling to meet with clients. I landed a column with Inc.com and launched a radio program, and then I initiated two weekly podcasts. (Just don't watch the first twenty episodes. Ouch!)

Dig your well by putting your plan in place. It may not include a column in a national magazine or a radio program, but just start by doing anything within your ability to build your relationships—and be sure they aren't only one-directional. My wife tells me I'm the nation's expert at working for free. What she means is, I have no boundaries. Ten to twenty requests weekly come to me from those who want some coaching, are asking for advice on writing a book or starting a company, are asking for a connection, or want me to appear on their Mastermind or in their community book club. I'm also asked regularly for advice on how to build a course or print a card deck, or how to find an agent or publicist. The list is endless.

And I say yes to every inbound request. Call me stupid. Call me a genius. But I never stop digging, and perhaps that's why my well has yet to run dry.

Lean on the Wisdom of Others

Of all the wisdom I've taken from my career with Franklin-Covey, the most profound has come from their former chief people officer, Todd Davis. He is a two-time *Wall Street Journal* bestselling author and one of the wisest sages from human resources you'll ever meet. He has a mantra he uses in his keynotes: "People are not an organization's most valuable asset. Rather, it's the relationships *between* those people that are in fact every organization's most valuable asset." That is true for each of us. Our relationships are what matter in our careers and in every other part of our lives.

Regardless of what business you're in, or what products or services you offer, your real value is found in the relationships you have with your colleagues, suppliers, and customers. You need to become an expert at building and strengthening your relationships. It's not easy for everyone, including me.

The following are some key traits of those who become experts at building relationships:

- They constantly assess what it's like to be in any kind of relationship with them by exercising a high level of self-awareness and making behavioral adjustments as needed.
- They take responsibility for their own actions and offer apologies without any excuses.
- They have an abundance mentality and help others even when not asked to.
- They give before they take or even ask.
- They check their natural jealousies and are genuinely happy for the success of others.
- They balance their speaking and listening ratio.
- They allow others to shine and compliment them on their wins.

- They are thoughtful with their reactions and regulate their emotions.
- They don't have a victim mentality and move beyond their norms to try new things.
- They are open to new ideas and reasonably accommodate the preferences of others.
- They set healthy boundaries that still allow for flexibility with others.
- They live intentionally balanced lives.
- They make and keep commitments.
- They behave themselves into a reputation of being trusted by others.

I invite you to reflect on how each of these points shows up in your life. And, just as importantly, grab your shovel and get to work. (By the way, if you reach out to me on any social platform I'm on, you now know I'll gladly accept!)

EXERCISE SETUP

Dig Your Well Before You're Thirsty

Hopefully at this point in the book you're aware of two recurring themes: (1) Becoming intentional about your career, and (2) Taking ownership over it. It's your responsibility. There is no blaming your leader or employer. No victim language or wishing others would accommodate your values or goals. Forgive me for channeling your parents, but keep the adage "If it's to be, it's up to me" top of mind.

My former leader at FranklinCovey, Bob Whitman, once said to me, "Thinking is a legitimate business activity." At first blush that may seem overly simplistic. But giving yourself the time and permission to be thoughtful, introspective, and intentional is the exact advice I'd invite you to follow. Especially as it relates to who you need to know. Need to call into action. Need to ask for a connection. Need to ask to throw you a lifeline.

Take a few minutes to assess your social networks and put some realistic growth targets in place.

LinkedIn
Current Number of Connections: ____________________
Growth in Ninety Days: ____________________

Facebook
Current Number of Friends: ____________________
Growth in Ninety Days: ____________________

X (Twitter)
Current Number of Followers: ____________________
Growth in Ninety Days: ____________________

TikTok
Current Number of Followers: ____________________
Growth in Ninety Days: ____________________

Instagram
Current Number of Followers: ____________________
Growth in Ninety Days: ____________________

YouTube
Current Number of Subscribers: ____________________
Growth in Ninety Days: ____________________

Personal Email Database
Current Number of Contacts: ____________________
Growth in Ninety Days: ____________________

Other

Current Number of [______]: ____________________

Growth in Ninety Days: ____________________

Part of networking is investing in other people. Use the following worksheet to aggregate your key insights and actions from all ten strategies while it's fresh in your mind. Do it with the intention of sharing it with the people in your network as well as reminding yourself of the work needed ahead. Remember that everyone will be at different points on their long-term plan, so individual insights and next steps will vary.

Dig Your Well Before You're Thirsty

Revisit each of the ten strategies. Record any key insights and the deliberate actions you will take to keep your career on course.

1 Know Your Professional Values

KEY INSIGHTS

KEY ACTIONS

2 Decide If You Are a Specialist or a Generalist

KEY INSIGHTS

KEY ACTIONS

3 Study Yourself

KEY INSIGHTS

KEY ACTIONS

4 Illustrate and Recalibrate Your Long-Term Plan

KEY INSIGHTS

KEY ACTIONS

5 Define and Build Your Brand

KEY INSIGHTS

KEY ACTIONS

6 Be Willing to Disrupt Yourself

KEY INSIGHTS

KEY ACTIONS

7 Take the Lead with Your Leader

KEY INSIGHTS

KEY ACTIONS

8 Do the Job You Were Hired For, Plus the One You Want

KEY INSIGHTS

KEY ACTIONS

9 Keep Your Ear to the Ground

KEY INSIGHTS

KEY ACTIONS

10 Dig Your Well Before You’re Thirsty

KEY INSIGHTS

KEY ACTIONS

CONCLUSION

Let's go back and do a high-level recap of the ten strategies we've discussed. However, before we proceed to review them, I'd like to remind you of a few important points.

- Most, if not all, of these exercises will not be accomplished in one sitting. They will require you to think, ponder, discover, uncover, explore, and perhaps even talk with people in various roles of your life. Don't take shortcuts. Invest as much time as necessary to think through answers to all of these valuable questions.
- Because some of these exercises may take you multiple days (or weeks) to fully flesh out, don't be crippled by that reality. Rather, simultaneously work through as many as is necessary to keep momentum.
- Be mindful of how many associates, friends, or family members you talk with to gather your insights, as people may become fatigued being asked to participate in too many conversations or activities. Gather your network from all parts of your life to ensure you have valuable and actionable information from which to operate. To that point, solicit feedback not only

from your biggest champions and supporters but also from your detractors.

- Finally, recognize that all of these exercises will evolve and change over time and will require you to revisit them, likely on an annual basis. Keep this book in an easy-to-reference location and view it more as a professional diary/journal that allows you to calibrate your thoughts, learning, and progress.

Strategy 1: Know Your Professional Values

The most intentional careers have a set of clearly defined personal and professional values. Ideally, they're both hierarchically ranked and form an acronym that helps you commit them to memory and align your behavior and time to them. And if you've made the investment in both sets of values, you'll benefit from immediately knowing when they're either in conflict or in harmony and how they complement each other. Trust me, as this is life-changing. Take your time selecting both sets of values. Don't rush it. I spent the better part of an entire weekend, alone and uninterrupted, doing so. And even though my life roles have changed drastically since then, interestingly, my values have not.

Strategy 2: Decide If You're a Specialist or a Generalist

One isn't better than the other. And yes, you can be both at the same time. Use this insight to determine how you might be experiencing the comparison conundrum and how you can release yourself from it.

Attention, Specialists: congratulations on your professional clarity. It will serve you well early. Be mindful of what adjustments you might need to make to ensure that if you want to make a pivot, you're set up well to do so.

Attention, Generalists: relax, all will be okay. You'll be able to use your broad skills and interests to your eventual advantage. Remember to work on knitting them all together so they serve you well later and aren't just a quilt of mismatched pieces.

Strategy 3: Study Yourself

Studying yourself is all about building self-awareness, which is arguably one of the most important investments you can make in your entire career and life. Remember, the top skills (aka *power skills*) every company is searching for are strong interpersonal capabilities, the talent to effectively communicate and collaborate with others, the ability to diffuse conflict when it arises, and the understanding of when to adjust your own style to accomplish these things. Your Team of Eight is now your own board of directors, but feel free to broaden your circle and ask as many people as possible these two vital questions:

"What's one thing I do that annoys you?"

"What's one thing I do that delights you?"

Most importantly, read Tasha Eurich's book *Insight: The Surprising Truth about How Others See Us, How We See Ourselves, and Why the Answers Matter More Than We Think.*

Strategy 4: Illustrate and Recalibrate Your Long-Term Plan

This is the central theme of the entire book and is the key differentiator between accidental and intentional careers.

What will be your TGI Fridays moment when you decide to finally take control over your career—looking not just around the corner but years and decades ahead? Remember, the path you articulate isn't solely one of forecasting but also one of backcasting. Your goal is to determine your ultimate career objective—yes, it may change—and put a stake in the ground for when you want to accomplish it, including compensation. Then you'll identify all the skills you'll need to master to land it, and do the same with every role before that one. This takes focus, discipline, dedication, and vision, but I assure you that those who have a plan—even if it's a weak plan or the plan changes—will out-execute everyone without one. Because you can't execute a plan that doesn't exist.

Strategy 5: Define and Build Your Brand

Every company, product, service, and person has a brand, either defined through neglect or formed intentionally. You get to decide which bodes better for you and your career. Personally, I'd vote against neglect. Your goal here is to eliminate dissonance between how you see your brand, how others see it, and what you want it to be. Similar to your work in building your Team of Eight, you'll want to identify three people in your life (ideally from both your personal and professional life) who will rise to the occasion and show the courage to tell you how they and others view your brand. I'd advise you to select people *not* from your Team of Eight, as they might start getting fatigued with all your questions. But then again, maybe not—only you will know best.

Strategy 6: Be Willing to Disrupt Yourself

Let this statement haunt you daily: "You're never in the room when your career is decided for you." I hope you find it as insulting as I do and take the steps to ensure it never describes your professional journey. Of course, you will find yourself in situations where you can't fully anticipate what is coming your way. Perhaps you're the department lead when your company is purchased by another—and your role becomes redundant and thus is eliminated. Or, alternatively, because you've worked to ensure the leaders in your company have seen you demonstrate skills beyond your current role, they not only keep you through the merger but promote you. Your commitment to yourself must include becoming comfortable with being uncomfortable. Stretch yourself. Intentionally place yourself in new and challenging situations. Forget impostor syndrome and fully admit to yourself that while you may have no idea what you're doing, you're going to turn it into a game and master it. Then do the same when the next "level" presents itself.

Strategy 7: Take the Lead with Your Leader

My controversial but well-vetted opinion is that not everyone should be a leader of people. This is true, in part, because the vast majority of people promoted into leadership excel at being an individual contributor. That's like being the fastest cashier in a grocery store. You scan the products quickly across the belt, make few mistakes, bag the groceries well, and then you're on to the next customer. You do an awesome job every day for eight hours a day in Lane 6, then, as a result, you get promoted to lead fifteen cashiers and the four back in the pharmacy whom you've never met. Now your job is scheduling, interviewing, firing, managing a payroll, coaching, giving feedback, and everything *but* jumping back into Lane 6 and bagging groceries. Though you still do that too, because that's what you know, and you convince yourself you're being helpful by pitching in. Only, given the bigger picture, you're not.

The moral of this example should be painfully obvious: there is zero correlation to the job you excelled at yesterday and what is now required of you as a leader today. Given this example, I invite you to remember a few things about your leader. First, they may be in over their head, and that doesn't automatically make them a bad person. They're likely just someone trying to do their best with the skills they have.

Second, just because someone is a leader doesn't mean they know how to provide feedback graciously, hold people accountable, or all the other requirements that come with leadership. Third, be gentle with your leader. Be kind. Be forgiving. Understand and empathize with the pressure they're under, and make yourself invaluable to them.

Finally—and most importantly for your intentional career —take control of the relationship to ensure they become your biggest champion.

Strategy 8: Do the Job You Were Hired For, Plus the One You Want

Ambition is great. I can smell it a building away. I look for it whenever I'm recruiting for my team. But more important than ambition is a demonstrable winning track record, a history of making and keeping commitments, and a bias for signing up for and overdelivering on not just current responsibilities but more. None of that can happen at the expense of what's expected from your current job. Job #1 is still and will always be job #1. Don't forget that as you stretch yourself to do more.

Strategy 9: Keep Your Ear to the Ground

Stay far from gossip. Don't participate in it, and if you get caught in the middle of it, graciously step out. Once you've clearly defined the difference between gossip and valuable information about what's happening inside your company, use it to your benefit. Identify trusted influencers to drill down to specifics around who, what, where, how, and when. Be sure to declare your intent. You're not trying to disingenuously manipulate them to get information, and you fully understand the concept of certain facts being on a need-to-know basis. After that, given their level of willingness, ask all the questions they're open to answering to help you best navigate and execute your next career move.

Strategy 10: Dig Your Well Before You're Thirsty

No matter what your career goals are, you're in the relationship business. I don't care if your focus is software, tulips, pizza, or some combination of them all. Whatever the product or service you're aligned with, you should always be striving to be an expert at building relationships. Assess your list of connections, especially those via your social media platforms, and use them to build and maintain mutually beneficial relationships. That way, your well will always be deep and never run dry.

BONUS STRATEGY

Own Your Development

This bonus strategy, Own Your Development, is correlated to the long-term map you've illustrated during Strategy 4: Illustrate and Recalibrate Your Long-Term Plan. If you recall, beneath each milestone on your map are six blank lines on which to write the skill sets needed for each career step in your future. I keep an evergreen trove of resources at **CareerOnCourseBook.com** for you to review as you invest in your own development. I advise you to correlate the professional development assets listed there with the skills that will set you up well for your next promotion.

I've taken the liberty of organizing my favorite books, podcasts, blog posts, videos, software, subscriptions, online training programs, and conferences in the hopes you might discover someone or something new to add to your lifelong pursuit of development. Some of these resources are career focused while others are personal investments in yourself, and I hope all are valuable to you as you seek to keep your career on course.

The most intentional careers are the ones in which people take full responsibility for every aspect of their professional journey, including their complete development. Visit **CareerOnCourseBook.com** frequently to benefit from what I hope becomes a go-to resource for you, your friends, your family, and your colleagues.

NOTES

Strategy 2 Decide If You're a Specialist or a Generalist

1. Kevin Leman, *The Birth Order Book: Why You Are the Way You Are* (Grand Rapids: Revell, 2015).

2. Indeed Editorial Team, "Generalist vs. Specialist: Which Is Better?," Indeed, April 26, 2021, https://www.indeed.com/career-advice/finding-a-job/generalist-vs-specialist.

3. David J. Epstein, *Range: Why Generalists Triumph in a Specialized World* (New York: Riverhead Books, 2020).

Strategy 5 Define and Build Your Brand

1. Adam Grant (@AdamMGrant), "Listen to the advice you give to others," Twitter post, September 19, 2019, https://twitter.com/adammgrant/status/1174772288924913665?lang=en.

Strategy 6 Be Willing to Disrupt Yourself

1. Whitney Johnson, *Disrupt Yourself: Putting the Power of Disruptive Innovation to Work* (Brookline, MA: Bibliomotion, 2015).

2. @dwyhapparel, "The way you react has been repeated thousands of times," Twitter post, February 11, 2020, https://twitter.com/dwyhapparel/status/1227275564706410496.

Strategy 7 Take the Lead with Your Leader

1. "Professional Flying Trapeze Training," Centre International des Arts en Mouvement, accessed January 19, 2023, http://www.artsenmouvement.fr/professional-flying-trapeze-training/.

2. CliftonStrengths, "An Introduction to the Competition CliftonStrengths Theme," Gallup, accessed May 16, 2023, https://www.gallup.com/cliftonstrengths/en/252191/competition-theme.aspx; CliftonStrengths, "An Introduction to the Significance CliftonStrengths Theme," Gallup, accessed May 16, 2023, https://www.gallup.com/cliftonstrengths/en/252341/significance-theme.aspx.

3. Andrew Francis-Tan and Hugo M. Mialon, "'A Diamond Is Forever' and Other Fairy Tales: The Relationship between Wedding Expenses and Marriage Duration," SSRN, September 27, 2014, https://papers.ssrn.com/sol3/papers.cfm?abstract_id=2501480.

4. Jack McCullough, "The Psychopathic CEO," *Forbes*, October 12, 2022, https://www.forbes.com/sites/jackmccullough/2019/12/09/the-psychopathic-ceo/?sh=274a172d791e.

5. David Rock, "Managing with the Brain in Mind," *Strategy + Business* 56 (Autumn 2009), https://www.strategy-business.com/article/09306.

Strategy 8 Do the Job You Were Hired For, Plus the One You Want

1. Edward M. Hallowell, *Shine: Using Brain Science to Get the Best from Your People* (Boston: Harvard Business Press, 2011).

SCOTT JEFFREY MILLER

SCOTT JEFFREY MILLER currently serves as FranklinCovey's senior advisor on thought leadership, leading the strategy and development of the firm's multiple podcasts and speaker's bureau, as well as leading the publication and distribution of their bestselling books, articles, columns, and interviews with their thought leaders.

Miller hosts the FranklinCovey-sponsored podcast *On Leadership with Scott Miller*, the world's largest and fastest growing leadership podcast, reaching more than six million people weekly, as well as the weekly podcast *C-Suite Conversations with Scott Miller*.

Miller is the author of the award-winning Mess to Success series, including *Management Mess to Leadership Success: 30 Challenges to Become the Leader You Would Follow* and *Marketing Mess to Brand Success: 30 Challenges to Transform Your Organization's Brand (and Your Own)*. He is the coauthor of the *Wall Street Journal* bestseller *Everyone Deserves a Great*

Manager: The 6 Critical Practices for Leading a Team, and the author of a ten-volume series, Master Mentors: 30 Transformative Insights from Our Greatest Minds, which features insights from his interviews with leading thinkers of our time including Seth Godin, Susan Cain, Daniel Pink, General Stanley McChrystal, Liz Wiseman, and many others.

In addition to supporting FranklinCovey's global thought leadership efforts, Miller has designed and launched the Career on Course coaching series to help leaders take their careers from accidental to intentional. He moderates Franklin Covey's Bookclub.com subscription series with world-renowned authors and is the cofounder of Gray + Miller, a new speakers agency launched in 2022 with the founder of Bookpal.com.

CONNECT WITH SCOTT

CareerOnCourseBook.com

Facebook @scottmillerjl

Instagram @ScottJeffreyMiller

LinkedIn ScottJeffreyMiller